Nancota Recv'd

W9-ANY-120

Better Homes and Gardens®

KITCHEN
PROJECTS
YOU CAN BUILD

BETTER HOMES AND GARDENS BOOKS

Editorial Director: Don Dooley
Executive Editor: Gerald M. Knox
Art Director: Ernest Shelton Asst. Art Director: Randall Yontz
Production and Copy Editor: David Kirchner
Building and Remodeling Editor: Noel Seney
Building Books Editor: Larry Clayton
Contributing Architectural Editor: Stephen Mead
Remodeling and Home Maintenance Editor: David R. Haupert
Building Ideas Editor: Douglas M. Lidster
Remodeling Ideas Editor: Dan Kaercher
Kitchens, Appliances, Home Management Editor: Joan McCloskey
Associate Editors: Kristelle Petersen, Cheryl Scott
Graphic Designers: Harijs Priekulis, Faith Berven,
Sheryl Veenschoten, Rich Lewis

© 1977 by Meredith Corporation, Des Moines, Iowa.
All Rights Reserved. Printed in the United States of America.
First Edition. First Printing.
Library of Congress Catalog Card Number: 77-74598
ISBN: 0-696-00250-7

CONTENTS

WORK/ SERVING CENTERS

Someplace in every home there's a wasted corner, an empty wall, or a few extra inches of floor space that could be put to good use. This section shows you how to make the best possible use of any area that's currently not earning its keep.

For instance, how would you like to trade a section of wall space for a wall-hung desk or storage cabinet? Or how about that bit of floor space in the middle of your kitchen? Improve it with a roll-around island that's both work surface and storage.

Since food preparation and service are the two most important functions of a kitchen, why not make the job easier with one of these nifty work or serving centers? They're inexpensive, and relatively easy to build with our drawings, materials specifications, and step-by-step instructions.

And if your carpentry skills are a little rusty, there's a basic information section in the back of the book that will help you.

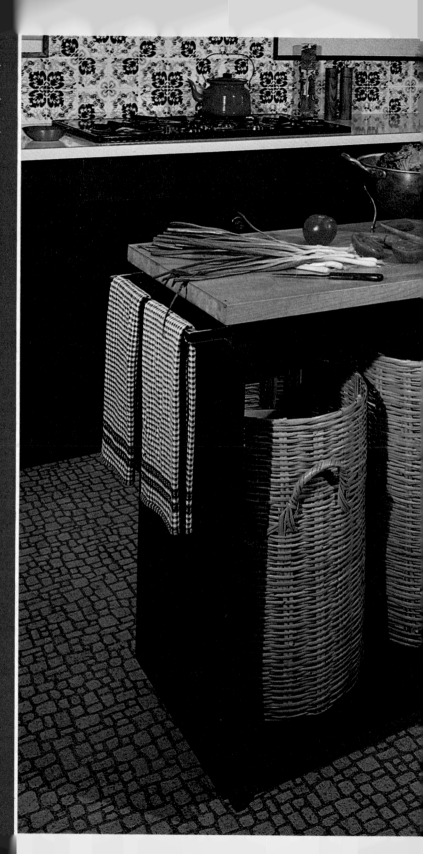

MOVABLE WORK ISLAND

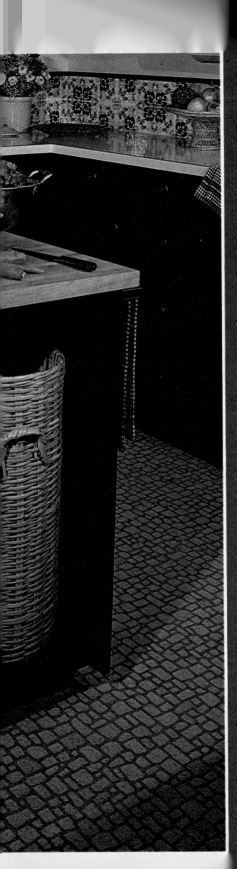

An extra work surface is always welcome, particularly when you can move it from place to place. Here's a roll-around island that's ideal for food preparation or service. A pair of towel bars act as push handles, and, just by inserting plastic wastebaskets, the two classy wicker hampers become hard-working trash receptacles or storage bins.

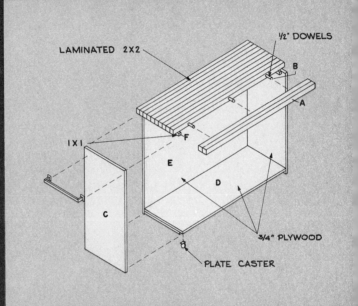

LAMINATED 2X2
½" DOWELS
B
A
1X1
F
E
D
C
3/4" PLYWOOD
PLATE CASTER

1 Using butt joints (see page 86), glue and screw together sides (C) and back (E) of unit. Glue and screw braces (F) ¼ inch up from bottom of back and sides and flush with top of sides. Attach bottom shelf (D) of unit.

2 For laminated top, drill holes in 2x2s (A) to accept ½-inch dowels (B). Apply glue to holes; fit dowels. Clamp together; let dry. (Option: Use an 18x32-inch cutting board for top.)

3 With glue and screws, fasten laminated top or cutting board to top of unit.

4 Fill all holes and exposed plywood edges with wood putty. Sand. Prime and paint unit desired color, using several coats with light sanding between each

coat. Or stain plywood to match the finish of your kitchen cabinets. Apply sealer, then at least two coats of varnish.

5 Screw on plate casters. Attach towel bars to each side of the unit.

Materials (18×32×36-in. unit):

¾-in. plywood—1½ shts.
- **C** 2 16½×33½ in.
- **D** 1 15¾×29 in.
- **E** 1 29×33½ in.
- **F** 4 14½ in.

2×2 fir—36 ft.
- **A** 12 32 in.

½-in. dowels—5 ft.
- **B** 3 16½ in.

Four plate casters, two 16-in. towel bars, glue, screws, and paint or stain and varnish.

SPACE-SAVER PLANNING CENTER

Where floor space is at a premium, build a wall-climbing unit like this one. It's a compact work/storage center that gives you a planning desk and open shelves that are perfect for cookbooks, home office records, or even extra kitchen gear and serving pieces. This handsome unit is made of oak and given a natural finish for the popular European look.

1 Mark intended heights of 1x4 ledgers (B) on 2x2 standards (A), then cut stopped dadoes (see page 87) in 2x2s. Glue and screw ledgers to standards.
2 Notch back corners of lower shelves (H) to fit around standards. Rest shelves on ledgers. Secure with glue and screws. Place 2x2 supports (C, D) between shelves and glue in position. Glue and screw top shelf to ledger and front supports.
3 Notch back corners of desk top (F) to fit around standards. Butt-join 1x2 strip (G) to front edge. Cut both ends of each 1x6 (E) at an angle to meet vertical standards and support desk top. Glue and screw opposite end of 1x6 to underside of desk. Rest back of desk top on ledger. Fasten 1x6 braces to vertical standards. Screw back of desk top to ledger.
4 Countersink all screws; fill with wood plugs. Finish unit.

Materials (84×41-in. unit):

2×2 oak or fir—24 ft.
A 2 83¼ in. **C** 4 9½ in.
D 2 16 in.
1×4—20 ft.
B 6 37 in.
1×6—4 ft.
E 2 21 in.
1×2—4 ft.
G 1 41 in.
¾-in. oak or fir veneer core plywood—¼ sht.
F 1 24×41 in.
(cut with grain)
1×12—14 ft.
H 4 41 in.
Glue, screws, wood filler, sealer, varnish and wood plugs.

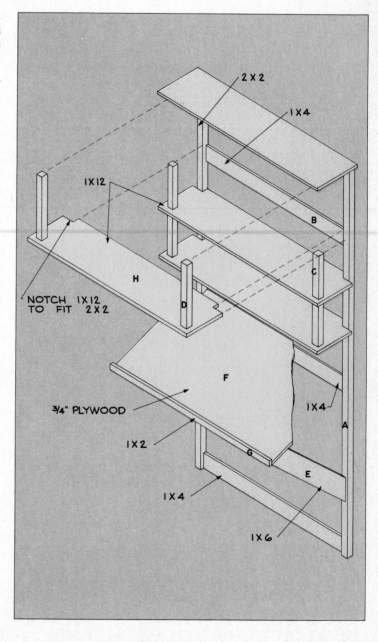

2 X 2
1 X 4
1 X 12
B
C
H
NOTCH 1X12 TO FIT 2 X 2
D
F
¾" PLYWOOD
1X4
A
1 X 2
G
E
1 X 4
1 X 6

VEST POCKET PLANNING CENTER

Any sliver of space in your kitchen can turn into an efficient mini-office with a wall-hung unit like this one. It's equipped with pigeon-holes, a drawer, and a drop-down front that doubles as a desk. Construct this compact center of 1x12s and plywood. Then stain it to blend with the wood of your kitchen, or paint on a sharp accent color.

1 Miter ends of unit top (A) (see page 88) and tops of side pieces (B). Rip 1x12 to 10¾ inches for bottom (C). Cut ¼-inch rabbets at back of top, bottom, and side pieces.

2 Determine placement of dividers (I, F). Make ¼-inch-wide dado (see page 87) in top and bottom pieces for full-size divider (F). Dado bottom piece for dividers under drawer unit (I). With glue and screws, fasten bottom and sides together, then attach back (D).

3 Make ¼-inch-wide dadoes in underside of drawer support bottom (H) to correspond with dadoes in bottom of unit. Miter drawer supports (G, H) where they join, and assemble with glue and screws. Glue dividers (F, I) to cabinet bottom and back. Secure support assembly to dividers (I) with glue, and to cabinet with glue and screws. Attach drawer guides (see page 92). Attach top of unit with glue and screws.

4 Assemble drawer as shown in sketch. Inset bottom and nail in place. Attach drawer guides.

5 Hinge ¾-inch plywood folding front (E) to bottom of unit.

6 Fill holes and exposed plywood edges with wood putty. Sand smooth. Paint unit at least two coats, or use stain and varnish (see page 96). Attach drawer pulls. Secure to wall (see page 90).

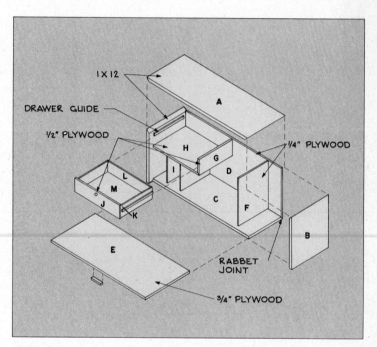

Materials (15×30×11½-in. unit):

1×12—8 ft.

A	1	30 in.
B	2	15 in.
C	1	28½ in.
		(rip to 10 ¾ in.)
G	1	4¾×9¾ in.
H	1	12¾×9¾ in.

¾-in. plywood—¼ sht.

E	1	13½×28½ in.

½-in. plywood—¼ sht.

J	1	4¼×12¼
K	2	4×9¼ in.
L	1	4×10 in.
M	1	9×10½ in.

¼-in. plywood—½ sht.

F	1	9¾×14 in.
I	2	9¼×9¾ in.
D	1	14×29 in.

Two drawer pulls, two hinges, two drawer guides, glue, screws, and paint or stain and varnish.

WELL-STACKED STORAGE/ SERVER

If bar supplies and bottles have been taking up space in your kitchen, this unit can move everything, conveniently and attractively, to another area of the house. The hutch top is designed with a drop-down shelf that serves as a bartop. And when it's covered with plastic laminate, you can use it without worrying about inevitable spills.

1 To construct the base, butt-join bottom (H), back (I), and side pieces (G), using glue and screws (see page 86). Mark the position of drawer guides and attach (see page 92). Attach top (F) to unit.

2 Cut ¼-inch rabbet ¼-inch wide (see page 87) on the bottom edge of drawer backs (L) and sides (K). Butt-join backs and sides of drawers using glue and screws. Glue and screw drawer bottoms (M) and fronts (J) in place. Attach guides to drawers.

3 To construct hutch top, butt-join sides (A), and top (B), and back (D) of the unit, using glue and screws. Position interior shelves (C). Fasten with glue and screws (for added strength, use dado joints; see page 87). Butt-join the bottom shelf (C) to the unit. Hinge drop-down shelf (E) as shown.

4 Fill all holes and plywood edges with wood putty. Sand all surfaces. Prime, then paint the unit, sanding lightly between coats. Leave the top surface of the bottom shelf and drop-down shelf unpainted. Cover these surfaces with plastic laminate. (Or if you prefer, use several coats of polyurethane varnish to make the surfaces impervious to moisture.) Attach magnetic catch to hold the drop-down shelf in closed position. Add drawer pulls, doorknob, and metal trim plates to front surface of hutch.

Materials (to build a 36½×30×20-in. base unit and a 42½×30×14-in. hutch):

¾-in. plywood—3½ shts.

B	1	30×14 in.	**F**	1	30×20 in.
A	2	41¾×14 in.			
C	3	28½×13¼ in.			
D	1	41¾×28½ in.			
E	1	28½×14 in.			
G	2	35¾×20 in.			
H	1	28½×20 in.			
I	1	28½×35¾ in.			
J	3	11⅝×28½ in.			
K	6	11⅝×18½ in.			
L	3	11⅝×26 in.			

¼-in. plywood—¾ sht.

M	3	18×26½ in.

One piano hinge, three drawer pulls metal tabs, glue, screws, paint, plastic laminate, contact cement, doorknob, magnetic catch, and drawer guides.

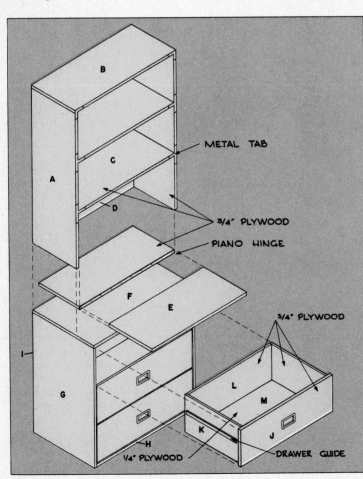

METAL TAB

¾" PLYWOOD

PIANO HINGE

¾" PLYWOOD

DRAWER GUIDE

¼" PLYWOOD

ROLL-AROUND BUFFET CABINET

Often, uncramping a kitchen means relocating extra equipment—and functions. Here's a roll-around cart that takes the squeeze out of kitchen storage. Use the roomy cabinet space for storing serving pieces or dishes. And the plastic laminate-covered top features a fold-up leaf to make a serving area large enough for a smorgasbord.

1 With butt joints (see page 86), assemble cabinet sides, back (H), and bottom (G) using glue and screws. Add 1x2 (I) at top of cabinet front. Attach shelf supports. Hinge doors (J) (see page 93).

2 Using butt joints, glue and screw together four 1x3s (C, D) to form unit's base. Add braces (E). Position cabinet on base, allowing toe-space at the front edge. Secure with glue and screws.

3 Glue plastic laminate to top and sides of top pieces (A, B) and hinge together. Glue assembly to top of cabinet. Add drop-leaf support, shelf brackets, and door pulls. Attach plate casters to the base of the unit. Paint the color of your choice.

Materials (to build a 30×18× 30-in. unit):

1¼-in. plywood—½ sht.
  A 1 30×18 in.
  B 1 12×18 in.

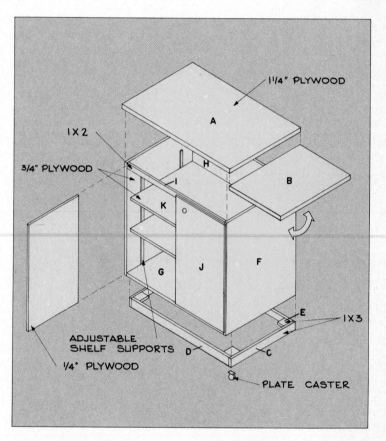

1¼" PLYWOOD

1 X 2

3/4" PLYWOOD

A
H
I
B
K
J
F
G

ADJUSTABLE SHELF SUPPORTS

D

E

1X3

C

¼" PLYWOOD

PLATE CASTER

¾-in. plywood—1 sht.
  F 2 26×18 in.
  G 1 28½×18 in.
  H 2 28½×25¼ in.
  K 2 28×16½ in.
¼-in. plywood—½ sht.
  J 2 14⅝×25¼ in.
1×3—8 ft.
  C 2 16½ in.

D 2 28½ in.
E 4 2½ in.
1×2—3 ft.
  I 1 28½ in.

Plastic laminate and adhesive, four door hinges, one piano hinge, four shelf supports, brackets, four plate casters, drop-leaf support, two door pulls, glue, screws, and paint.

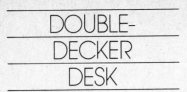

DOUBLE-DECKER DESK

Two wall-hung work centers are twice as practical as one, and this matched pair will stack up to anything around. Build them from ¾-inch plywood. Our top unit measures a formidable 30x30 inches, and the 20-inch-deep bottom unit is 24x30 inches.

1 Using butt joints (see page 86), glue and screw together sides (A) and back (B) of top unit. Position shelves (C). Glue and screw in place.
2 Butt-join sides (D), back (E), and bottom (F) of bottom unit. Fasten with glue and screws. Position top shelf (G) down 3 inches from top edge of unit. Glue and screw in place. Position the 3x6-inch divider pieces (H) to divide the shelf space into four equal parts. Glue and screw in place.
3 Place the 3x19 ¼-inch divider (I) so that it divides the bottom desk surface in half. Glue and screw the divider in place. Place the second 28½x19¼-inch piece on top to form the writing surface. Glue and screw this piece in place.
4 Fill all holes with wood putty. Apply veneer stripping to all of the exposed plywood edges. Prime the unit and paint the color of your choice, sanding lightly between coats.

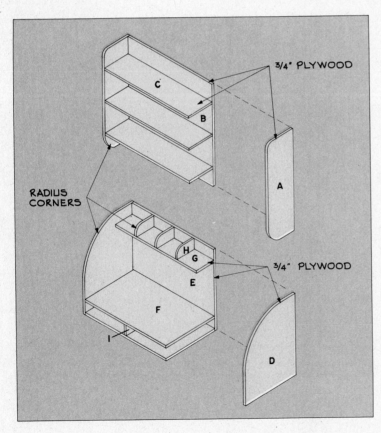

RADIUS CORNERS

¾" PLYWOOD

¾" PLYWOOD

Materials for a 30×30×9-inch top unit:

¾-in. plywood—1 sht.
- **A** 2 9×30 in. (radius 2 corners)
- **B** 1 28½×30 in.
- **C** 3 28½×8¼ in.

For 24×30×20-inch bottom unit:

¾-in. plywood—1 sht.
- **D** 2 24×20 in. (16-in. radius)
- **E** 1 28½×24 in.
- **F** 2 28½×19¼ in.
- **G** 1 28½×6 in.
- **H** 3 6×3 in. (radius corners)
- **I** 1 3×19¼ in.

Glue, ¾-in. veneer stripping, screws, and paint or stain.

CABINET/ CLOSET ORGANIZERS

The value of any closet or cabinet is judged by two things—how much you can store inside and how easily you can get at all the things you store. Just being able to toss your belongings somewhere and close the door on them isn't good enough. You should also have everything you need in easy reach.

That's what this section is all about—organizers to efficiently hold everything you put away, and keep it right at your fingertips when you need it. We'll show you how to customize your existing closets and cabinets, plus how to build specialized cabinets anywhere you need but don't have them.

Overall sizes and material lists given here refer to the units shown in the photos. You'll probably want to adapt these ideas to fit your particular space, in which case you'll simply increase or decrease appropriate dimensions and material requirements.

For general construction tips, refer to the "how-to basics" section starting on page 85. It explains all you need to know to tackle any job like a pro.

BUFFET BEHIND DOORS

A closet's usefulness increases several hundred percent when you customize its interior. Here, we equipped a 5-foot-wide, 2-foot-deep closet space with a buffet counter, shelves, drawers, and compartments for vertical storage of trays or large platters. Use this idea and adjust the measurements to fit whatever space you'd like put to better use. You'll be glad you did.

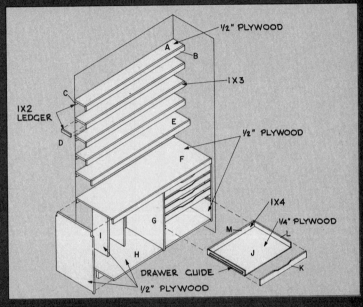

1 Attach ledgers (C, D) for top shelves to back and sidewalls. Glue and screw trim pieces (B) to shelves (A, E). Attach trimmed shelf boards to ledgers.

2 Nail base supports (N) to floor. Notch top and bottom of sides and center divider (G) to align flush with top trim and lower edge of bottom shelf (H). Position center divider (G) and screw through bottom (H). Attach side pieces (G) to wall. Glue and screw trim (B) to top (F).

3 Nail ledger (C) to back wall for top (F). Attach top to ledger and cabinet sides. Secure dividers (I) with glue and screws.

4 Cut notch in drawer fronts (K) for pulls. Construct drawers (J, K, L, M) (see page 92). Attach drawer guides. Fill all holes, sand unit and finish as desired.

Materials (for storage area contained in 2×5-ft.-wide space):

½-in. plywood—4 shts.

A	4	60×6 in.
E	1	60×8 in.
F	1	60×21 in.
G	3	32×21¾ in.
H	1	60×21 in.
I	2	10×31½ in.

¼-in. plywood—1 sht.

| J | 5 | 26⅜×21 in. |

1×3—30 ft.

| B | 6 | 60 in. |

1×2—34 ft.

| C | 6 | 60 in. | D | 10 | 4½ in. |

1×4—42 ft.

K	5	28⅞ in.
L	10	21 in. (milled to 3¼ in.)
M	5	26⅜ in. (milled to 3¼ in.)

2×4—10 ft.

| N | 2 | 60 in. |

Drawer guides, glue, nails, screws.

PULL-OUT CABINET SHELVES

The back corners of base cabinets are often wasted space, primarily because they're hard to get at. But this simple remodeling project puts them in easy reach with glide-outs that combine the best features of both shelves and drawers.

1 Remove cabinet doors. Remove existing shelving and supports.

2 Dado (see page 87) drawer sides (D) and back (C) to receive bottom (B); secure. Butt-join (see page 86) back and side pieces, using glue and screws. Glue and screw supports (E) to underside of drawer bottom. Cut hand pulls in drawer fronts (A). With glue and screws attach fronts to finished drawers.

3 Install drawer guides (see page 92) on inside sidewalls of cabinet. Attach drawer guides to sides of drawers. Insert drawers.

4 With piano hinges, hinge doors (see page 93) in pairs. Hinge doors to cabinet.

5 Fill all holes. Sand unit and paint or stain as desired.

Materials (dimensions for drawers in existing cabinet unit with interior width of 52 in.):

³/₄-in. plywood—1 sht.
  B 2 20×50 in.
1×4—24 ft.
  A 2 52 in.   **D** 4 20½ in.
  C 2 49½ in.
1×2—10 ft.
  E 6 20 in.
Heavy-duty side-mount drawer guides, two piano hinges, glue, screws, four magnetic catches, and paint or stain.

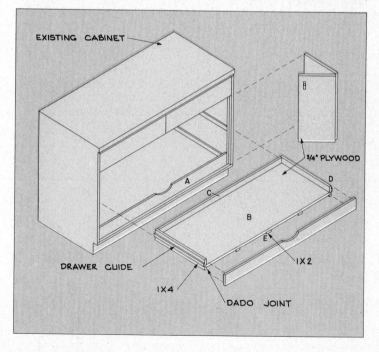

EXISTING CABINET

¾" PLYWOOD

DRAWER GUIDE

1X4

DADO JOINT

1X2

DOOR-HUNG POTS 'N' PANS STORAGE

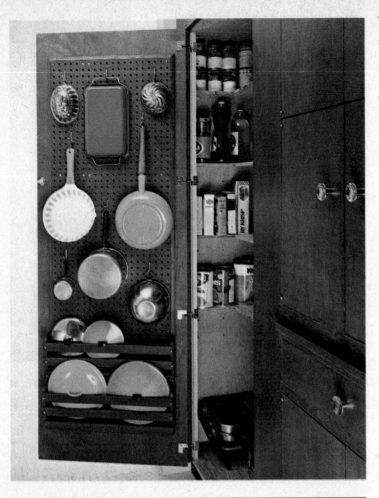

Bulky pots and pans can clobber even the best planned kitchen storage scheme. So if you're tired of chasing loose lids around the cupboards and stooping to stack pans in a cabinet, try this efficient pegboard organizer.

Attached to the back of a cabinet door, it provides hanging space for pans while racks take care of their lids.

1 Bevel outside edges of the four frame pieces (B, C). Miter (see page 88) corners and assemble frame using glue and screws.

2 Cut rack side pieces (D) so front edge slopes in to 2 inches at the bottom. Bevel the back edges to fit the frame. Glue and screw bottoms (F) and slats (E) onto side pieces (D).

3 Screw pegboard (A) to assembled frame. Attach the two lid racks by screwing through the frame from the back side. Paint or stain as desired. Screw to fit unit to inside of cabinet door. (NOTE: Shelves may have to be trimmed to allow for storage unit when door is closed.)

Materials (for a unit to fit a 24×60 in. door):

1/8-in. pegboard—1 sht.
  A 1 18½×50½ in.
1×2—12 ft.
  B 2 20 in.   **C** 2 52 in.
1×4—4 ft.
  D 4 9½ in.
½-in. plywood—¼ sht.
  E 6 2×20 in. **F** 2 2×18½ in.
Glue, screws, paint or stain, and pegboard hooks.

Diagram labels: EXISTING DOOR, BEVELED 1X2, PEGBOARD, ½" PLYWOOD, 1X4, A, B, C, D, E, F

CLEAN-UP CLOSET ORGANIZER

When it comes to household cleaning supply closets, you can have one big, disorganized mess that's a close second to Fibber McGee's—or you can have a neat, orderly closet with a place for every-thing and everything in its place. If you opt for the latter, build this compartmented storage unit that's complete with a towel bar and even a bin for paper bags. Then give it class with color.

1 Mark the placement of top shelf (K) and nail ledgers (J, M, N) to the sidewalls of closet. Mark placement of lower shelves (C, D) and nail ledgers (I) in place.
2 With butt joints (see page 86), assemble shelves (B) and verticals (A) of side unit, using glue and screws. Place in closet and nail to the sidewall.
3 Miter (see page 88) bottom edge of bin (E) to fit bottom (F). Join with glue and screws. Toe-nail assembled bin to wall; glue and screw to vertical (A). Screw shelf (D) to ledger and vertical (A).
4 With butt joints, attach side pieces (H) to long shelf (C). Place shelf (G) on top. Glue and screw. Rest shelf assembly on verticals (A); screw into ledger (I). Attach top shelf (K) to ledgers. Screw on shower rod brackets and insert dowel (L).

Materials (for unit to fit inside 36-in.-wide, 15-in.-deep closet):

¾-in. plywood—1 sht.
  A 2 12×48 in.
  B 3 12×14 in.
  C 1 12×36 in.
  K 1 14×36 in.
  D 1 12×20½ in.
  E 1 10×20½ in.
  F 1 4×20½ in.
  G 1 12×15½ in.
  H 2 12×10 in.
1×2—2 ft.
  I 2 12 in.
1×4—8 ft.
  J 1 15 in. (or depth of closet)
  M 1 12 in.
  N 1 34½ in.
1-in. dowel—3 ft.
  L 1 34½ in.
Glue and shower rod brackets.

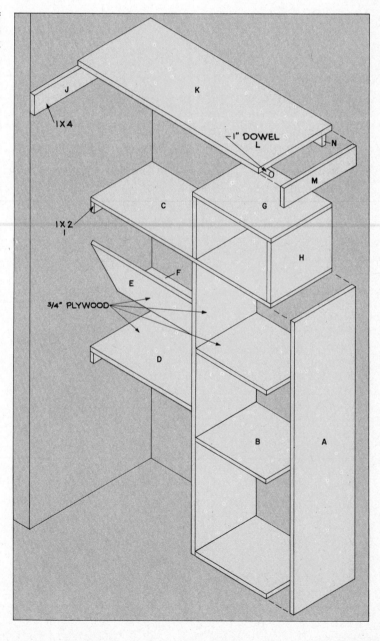

UNDER-SINK MESS ERADICATORS

These two easy-to-build units can make the difference between order or chaos in an under-the-sink cabinet. On one side there's sloped shelf storage for canned goods. On the other side are vertically divided spaces for storing trays. A sliver of extra space holds paper bags, and directly under the disposer is a plastic pull-out drawer to keep cleaning supplies in easy reach.

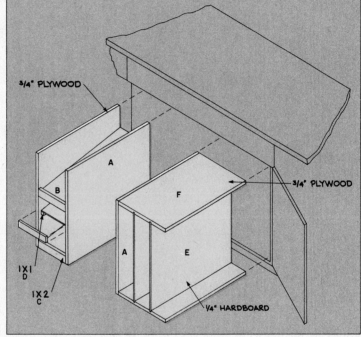

1 To construct divider section, dado (see page 87) top and bottom (F) to receive verticals (E). Using butt joints (see page 86), assemble sides (A) and top and bottom (F) with glue and nails. Coat top and bottom edges of verticals (E) with glue and position in dadoed pieces (F).

2 To construct can storage unit, determine spacing and slope of shelves (B) on side pieces (A). Attach ledgers (D) to sides using glue and nails. Butt-join 1x2 facing strips (C) to sides forming lips for shelves. Glue and nail shelves (B) to ledgers (D).

3 To finish both sections, countersink all nails. Fill holes and exposed plywood edges with wood putty. Sand units and paint, using at least two coats. Place units in under-sink cabinet as shown in photo.

Materials (for storage and divider units in a 24-in.-deep, 28-in.-wide lower cabinet):

¾-in. plywood—1 sht.
  A 4 23×24 in.   **F** 2 23×12 in.
¼-in. hardboard—½ sht.
  B 3 6×26 in.   **E** 2 23×23 in.
1×2—2 ft.
  C 3 6 in.
1×1—14 ft.
  D 6 26 in.
Glue, nails, paint, and assembled sliding drawer unit.

LINEN STORAGE UNITS

Finding the tablecloth or place mats you want doesn't have to be a scavenger hunt through a crowded drawer. Here, a broom closet has been equipped with some cleverly designed "hangers" to keep tablecloths close by and—believe it or not—wrinkle-free. With the addition of horizontal plywood dividers to form slim shelves, the overhead cabinet becomes a handy place-mat storage area.

1 To construct horizontally divided storage space, nail ledgers (B) to sidewalls of existing cabinet. Sand shelves (A) and paint as desired.

2 Slip shelves in place on the ledgers. As an alternative to ledgers, recess adjustable shelf standards into sidewalls of the cabinet and support the plywood shelves with shelf clips.

3 To assemble the tablecloth rack, dado (see page 87) backers (C) to receive the hardboard supports (D). Dadoes should be placed every 2½ inches.

4 Dado 1x1 "nosing" (E) to slip over the hardboard supports (D). Sand 1x1s (E) to create rounded top edge.

5 Cut hardboard (D) so back edge length is 10 inches and front edge is 1½ inches. Glue "nosing" strips to hardboard supports, flush with front edges. Glue supports (D) into dadoes of backers (C).

6 Paint the unit if desired or leave it natural. Screw the unit in place in existing cabinet. (NOTE: the height of cabinets is not critical. If necessary, alter unit measurements to fit cabinet width and depth.)

Materials (for units in a 20-in.-wide, 18-in.-deep cabinet):

½-in. plywood—1 sht.
  A 5 20×18 in.
¼-in. hardboard—½ sht.
  D 6 17½×10 in.
1×1—24 ft.
  B 10 18 in.   **E** 6 17¼ in.
1×3—4 ft.
  C 2 20 in.
Glue, nails, screws, and paint.

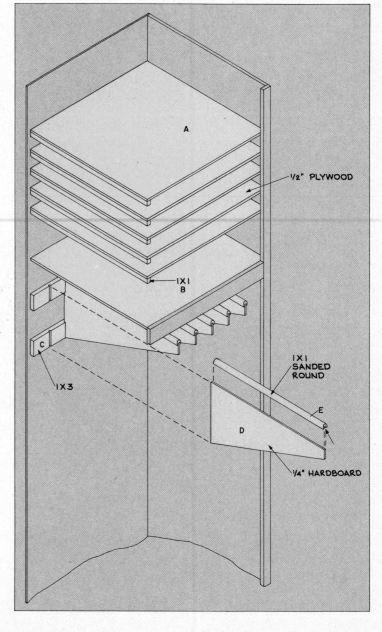

PULL-OUT PAN STORAGE

Hang-ups are nothing to be ashamed of when they're your cooking utensils. By customizing a stock 6-inch cabinet with a pull-out unit, you can hang pots, pans, measuring cups— anything that's hangable. This quick-and-easy project is simply a pegboard panel framed with 1x2s and attached to a cabinet door. Drawer guides make the pulling-out a cinch.

1 Cut ⅛-inch dadoes (see page 87) ¼ inch deep in center of frame pieces (A, B) inside edges. Cut miter corners (see page 88) on frame pieces.
2 Insert pegboard (C) in dadoes and join frame, using glue and screws. Attach assembly to door, using one piece of angle iron on each side of frame section that butts door. Screw into frame and door every 6 inches.
3 Install drawer guides.
4 Countersink screw heads, fill holes and sand. Stain frame to match cabinet. Varnish.

Materials (for a cabinet opening 29×5×24-in. deep):

1×2—8 ft.
  A 2 29 in.   **B** 2 18 in.
⅛-in. pegboard—¼ sht.
  C 1 26½×15½ in.
Two drawer guides, two pieces of angle iron, glue, screws, stain, varnish, and pegboard hooks.

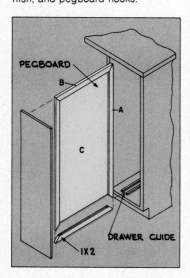

PEGBOARD
B
A
C
1×2
DRAWER GUIDE

TWIXT-STUD STORAGE

This clever cabinet idea converts most any chunk of wall surface into out-of-sight shelf space. To put hidden stud space to work for you, outfit the area with shelves and add a shutter door as a cover up. For a slick look, treat the back surface to a wall covering. We've used burlap, but vinyl or adhesive-backed paper would work as well.

1 Locate the studs in the area where you want your storage. Be sure space between studs does not contain pipes, ducts, or wiring. Knock out the wall surface between studs. Glue wall covering to back wall if desired.
2 Nail ledgers (B) directly to the studs or build an enclosing frame of 1x4s and attach ledgers to the frame. Secure shelves (A) to ledgers with glue and nails.
3 Install hinges (see page 93) on door (C). Attach to unit.
4 Fill all holes with wood putty. Sand well and paint or stain as desired.

Materials (for a 16×48-in. unit):
1×4—8 ft.
  A 5 14½ in.
1×2—4 ft.
  B 10 3½ in.
Two hinges, wall covering (optional), glue, paint or stain, and 1 16×48-in. shutter door (**C**).

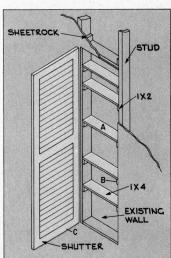

CABINET CLUTTER CUTTERS

A little extra planning of a cabinet's interior space pays off big when it comes to better storage. This pair of built-in cabinet organizers increases storage while also adding convenience and efficiency to the kitchen. So see if you can't fit units like this into your kitchen scheme.

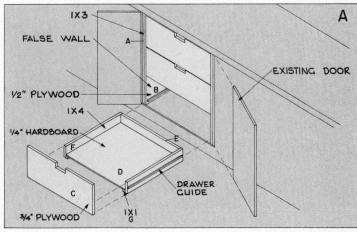

1 For unit A, build false wall (A, B) at cabinet sides.
2 Butt-join drawer sides (F) and back (E). Flush nailers (G) at bottom of sides. Attach bottom (D). Cut pull notch in drawer front (C). Attach. Add drawer guides.

Materials: (for unit in 30×30×24-in. interior):

½-in. plywood—½ sht.
  B 2 23×30 in.
¾-in. plywood—½ sht.
  C 3 10×27½ in.
¼-in. hardboard—½ sht.
  D 3 25×21½ in.
1×4—18 ft.
  E 3 25 in.   **F** 6 22¼ in.
1×3—16 ft.
  A 6 30 in.
1×1—12 ft.
  G 6 21½ in.
Drawer guides, glue, and screws.

1 For unit B, butt-join (see page 86) nailers (H, I). Screw pegboard sides (J) to nailers.
2 Miter corners (see page 88)

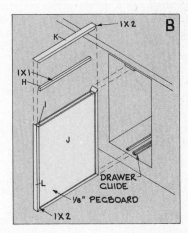

on frame pieces (K, L). Assemble with glue and screws. Add drawer guides.

Materials (24-in.-high interior):

⅛-in. pegboard—½ sht.
  J 2 21¾×21½ in.
1×2—10 ft.
  K 2 23 in.   **L** 2 23¼ in.
1×1—8 ft.
  H 2 20 in.   **I** 2 21¾ in.
Drawer guides, glue, and screws.

EASY ACCESS STORAGE

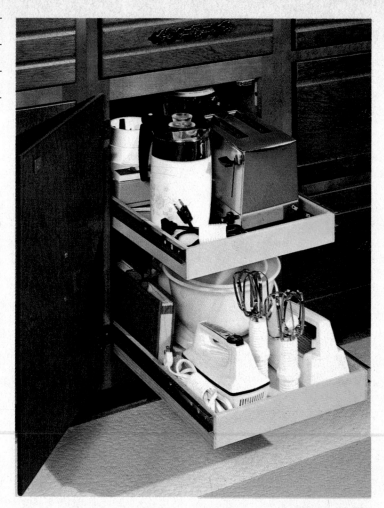

Not having enough kitchen storage is definitely a problem—but having the space and not being able to utilize every inch is nearly as frustrating. For instance, those far reaches of base cabinets are often graveyards for things you don't use just because you can't get at them. But you can solve that problem with these simple-to-build pullouts that put even back corners within easy reach. Build these drawers from 1x4s and attach metal drawer guides for smooth operation.

1 Cut ¼-inch rabbet (see page 87) at inside bottom edge of drawer sides (B) and back (C). Butt-join (see page 86) side and back pieces (B, C) using glue and screws. Fit bottom (D). Glue and screw to drawer frame. Attach drawer front (A).

2 Fill all of the holes with wood putty. Sand drawers well and finish as desired. If you plan to stain the unit, use filler, stain, sealer, and at least two coats of varnish (see page 96).

3 Install drawer guides (see page 92 for details) on sides of drawers and inside of cabinet.

Materials (for 2 drawers in a cabinet 14 in. wide and 24 in. deep):

1×4—12 ft.
  A 2 13 in.   **C** 2 11½ in.
  B 4 20 in.
¼-in. hardboard—¼ sht.
  D 2 12×19½ in.
Metal drawer guides, glue, screws, and paint or stain.

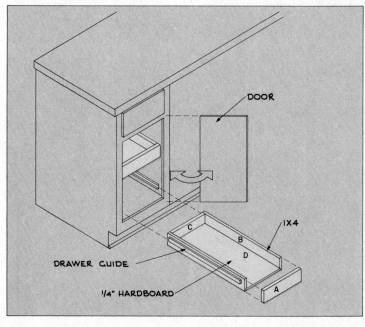

TOP-DECK KITCHEN WINE RACK

The space above a refrigerator can be put to good use with a wine rack like the one shown here. This unit is designed with an insulated bottom and back so heat from the appliance won't affect your wine.

1 Adjust height and width measurements to fit existing sidewalls in enclosure.

2 Butt-join (see page 86) the back and bottom (E, C), using glue and screws. Put the foam board insulation in place. Butt-join the sub-back (F) to the sub-bottom (D). Attach the top (G) as shown in the drawing.

3 Cut divider pieces (I) to appropriate lengths. Cut notches as shown in drawing. Paint sections of wine rack. Assemble divider section and slip into rack frame. Place wine rack in opening above refrigerator.

4 Add trim (A, B) and finish with cove molding (H). Paint the entire unit.

Materials (for a 32×18×13-in. wine rack):

¹/₂-in. plywood—3 shts.
- **C,E** 2 12½×32 in.
- **D** 1 11½×32 in.
- **F** 1 15½×32 in.
- **G** 1 13×32 in.
- **I** 16 11-in.-wide dividers cut to appropriate lengths

1×4—6 ft.
- **A** 2 29 in.

1×2—2 ft.
- **B** 2 18 in.

³/₄-in. cove molding—3 ft.
- **H** 1 32 in.

1-in. foam board insulation, glue, screws, nails, and paint.

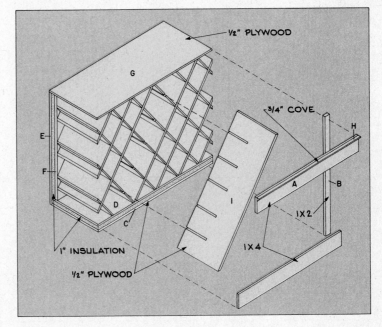

½" PLYWOOD

¾" COVE

1×2

1×4

1" INSULATION

½" PLYWOOD

CLASSY CATCH-ALL CLOSET

When your home isn't blessed with an abundance of storage space, you have to add it. And no space works harder than the sliver of wall you devote to a compartmented closet like this one. Outfit yours with a fold-down ironing board, or use the newly created storage space for canned goods, cleaning supplies, or anything else that needs stashing.

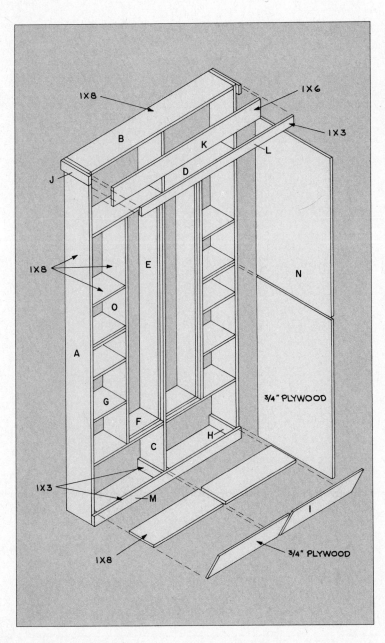

1 Butt-join (see page 86) sides (A), top and bottom (B), using glue and screws. Place unit against wall and nail to floor. For more strength, dado shelves adding ½ inch to shelf length and add a ledger at top of unit and screw into wall studs.
2 Add middle vertical (C) and ledgers (H). Attach long shelves (D) to the unit. Glue and screw verticals (O) in place. Rip inner box pieces (E, F) to 7 inches and miter (see page 88) corners. Attach to outer frame. Butt-join outer shelves (G) to unit (use two thicknesses at point where upper and lower doors meet).
3 Add top trim (J, K). Attach trim piece (L) to 1x6 (K). Glue and nail bottom trim (M) in place.
4 Angle bottom edge of bin fronts (I). Attach to unit. Hinge doors (N) (see page 93).

Materials (for an 8¼×96×48-inch unit):

1×8—96 ft.
A	2	96 in.	**F**	4	12 in.
B	2	46½ in.			
C	1	94½ in.			
D	6	22⅞ in.			
G	10	10⅛ in.			
O	2	61½ in.			
E	4	60 in.			

1×3—18 ft.
H	4	7½ in.	**M**	1	48 in.
J	2	8¼ in.			
L	1	49½ in.			

1×6—4 ft.
K	1	48 in.

¾-in. plywood—1½ shts.
I	2	8×22⅞ in.
N	4	23¹⁵/₁₆×43¹⁵/₁₆

Eight pivot hinges, glue, nails, screws, paint or stain.

FREE-STANDING STORAGE COLUMN

It's a snap to keep cleaning supplies organized and easy to find with a storage workhorse like this floor-to-ceiling cabinet. Its attractive planked walls are formed by gluing pine boards together—and its unique design gives you the convenience of an "automatic" cleaning rag dispenser. Use this handy unit in a corner, or as a freestanding column divider to break up large room areas.

1 Glue and clamp together boards (A) to form sides. Nail on nailers (J). Attach nailers (H, I) to ceiling. Nail sides to ceiling nailers. Nail bottom nailers (J) to floor.

2 Cut 6-inch-radius semicircle in bin front (E). Nail shelves (F, G), top rail (B), and bin front (E) in place. Hinge doors (C, D) to unit. Add door pulls.

Materials (24×24×96-in. unit):

¾-in. plywood—1 sht.

B	1	22½×9 in.
C	1	22½×21 in.
D	1	22½×66 in.
E	1	22½×12 in.
F	1	22½×22½ in.
G	1	22½×23¼ in.

1×8 pine—96 ft.

A	12	96 in. (cut 6 in. wide)

1×2—16 ft.

H,J	6	22½ in.	I 2	21 in.

Five cabinet hinges, glue, nails, and door pulls.

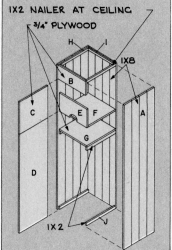

1X2 NAILER AT CEILING
¾" PLYWOOD
H I
1X8
B
C
E F
A
G
D
1X2
J

SWINGING STORAGE PANTRY

Here's how to turn an existing closet or appliance enclosure into one of the most usable, practical shelf storage units around. The door rack snuggles into the center of the U-shaped shelves, putting everything in clear sight and easy reach. And if you don't have a cabinet or closet waiting to be converted, simply frame one in.

1 Nail ledgers (B, C) to back and sidewalls. Cut shelves (A) as shown. Nail to ledgers (B, C). Nail base (E, F) to floor. Attach bottom shelf (D).

2 Butt-join door rack (I, J) as shown. Attach rails (K).

3 Cut 24x63 in. opening in door (G). Glue on front panel (H). Screw rack to door. Hinge door.

Materials (for 36×12 in. unit):

¾-in. plywood—2 shts.

A,D	8	12×36 in.	**G**	1	30×80 in.

½-in. plywood—1 sht.

H	1	30×80 in.

1×4—30 ft.

E	2	36 in.	**F**	2	10½ in.
I	2	63 in.	**J**	6	22½ in.

1×2—36 ft.

B	7	36 in.	**C**	14	11¼ in.

Screen bead—12 ft.

K	6	24 in.

Two door hinges, glue, screws, nails, and paint or stain.

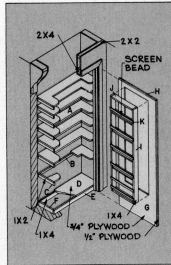

ADAPTABLE SHELVING UNITS

There's probably no room in your home that needs shelves as much as your kitchen does. Whether your storage problem involves dishes, linens, cookware, canned goods, or cookbooks—the solution is the right kind of shelves.

Here's a section of kitchen shelving to meet most every storage need. These units range in size from slim little see-through shelves in front of a window—to shelves that cover a whole wall. Most of these designs are easily adapted to your particular kitchen space and function. So browse through them and find the ones most apt to ease your storage crunch.

No matter what your degree of carpentry expertise, there's a project here for you. And if you need a quick refresher course in building basics, turn to the back of the book.

To begin, analyze your storage requirements. Then pick the units that do the job best. Alter the materials, dimensions, or finish and any one of these projects will look like a custom design created especially for your home.

SEE-THROUGH KITCHEN CUPBOARD

Why waste the space over your kitchen work counter? You can use it for ceiling-hung shelves. Glass doors on both sides of this unit give the look of open shelving, but keep the contents clean and accessible. And the cabinet is roomy enough to store all your dishes and glassware. So if your kitchen is short on shelves—try this sure-fire winner.

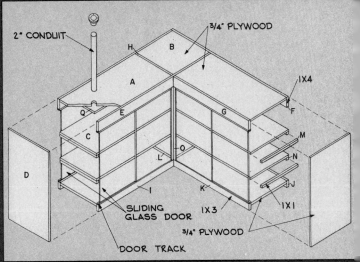

1 Butt-join (see page 86) L-shaped top section (A, B, E, H, G, F). Use glue and screws.
2 Butt-join L-shaped bottom section (A, B, I, L, K, J) as shown in sketch. Attach end panels (D).
3 Glue and screw nailers (O, M) and ledgers (N) to underside of L-shaped shelves (C). Attach ledgers (N) to wall side only.
4 Position shelves within interior of cabinet. Glue and screw through nailers (O, M) into end panels (D). Attach the corner 1x1 strip (P).
5 Attach flange to ceiling and install flange and fastening plate (Q) to underside of cabinet top. Attach cabinet to wall, screwing through ledgers (F, N, J) into studs. To support left section, attach conduit to flanges on cabinet top and ceiling.
6 Install track for glass doors.

7 Fill holes and plywood edges. Sand. Finish. Install doors.

Materials (for a unit 46×46×36 inches high):

¾-in. plywood—1½ shts.

A	4	14½×29¼ in.
B	2	14½×14½ in.
C	2	15¼×44½×44½ in.
		(rip one leg to 14½ in.)
D	2	16×30 in.
Q	1	6×6 in.

1×4—16 ft.

E	2	44½ in.	G	1	29¼ in
F	1	45¼ in.	H	1	14½ in

1×3—16 ft.

I	2	44½ in.	K	1	29¼ in
J	1	45¼ in.	L	1	14½ in

1×1—16 ft.

M	4	14½ in.	O	1	24 in.
N	2	44½ in.			

Glue, screws, tempered glass doors, track, 2-inch conduit, two pipe flanges, and paint, or stain and varnish.

ISLAND OF SHELVES AND DRAWERS

A bank of open shelves creates an island of efficiency in any kitchen. And the one shown here doesn't stop at just shelf space. It provides four roomy drawers for storage of silver or table linens— **plus an expanse of butcher block large enough to act as a serving counter. Major parts are made of laminated wood and shelves and drawer fronts are covered with plastic laminate for easy up-keep.**

1 Adjust height of verticals for ceiling. Drill holes in pieces to be laminated (A, B, D, E). Glue and insert dowels (C, F) in ends (A), horizontal (B), verticals (D, E). Clamp; let dry.

2 Cut dado (see page 87) in upper section verticals (A, E) to receive shelf supports. Install.

3 Drill holes in laminated members to receive joining dowels (S). Glue and insert dowels. Clamp together and dry. Attach to ceiling.

4 Glue and toenail base (G, H).

5 Glue and screw bottom shelves (I, J) to base (G, H). Glue and toenail remaining lower shelves (I, J) in place.

6 Cut ¼-inch rabbet (see page 87) in drawer sides (L) and back (M). Assemble (K, L, M, N) as in sketch.

7 Glue and screw nailers (P, hidden 32-in. center nailer) to back facers (O, hidden center piece). Attach assembled nailers and facers to frame.

8 With glue and screws, butt-join (see page 86) dividers (R) to center back facers. Dado drawer stop (Q) to receive divider (R) (see detail). Nail and glue.

9 Glue on vinyl cove base. Install drawer guides. Glue plastic laminate on shelves and drawer fronts; add pulls. Install shelves with clips. Finish.

Materials (for 25½×70×84-in. unit):

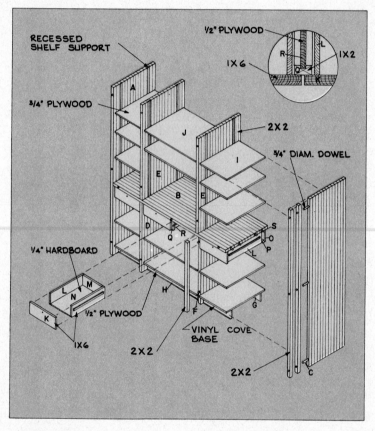

2×2—510 ft.

A	34	84 in.	**D** 34	34½ in.
B	17	67 in.	**E** 34	48 in.

¾-in. dowel—38 ft.

C 9 25½ in.

F 8 23½ in.
S 24 2 to 3 in.

½-in. plywood—½ sht.

G 4 4×16 in.
H 2 4×32 in.
R 1 5¼×21⅝ in.

¾-in. plywood—2 shts.

I 10 16×22⅞ in.
J 4 32×22⅞ in.

¼-in. hardboard—1 sht.

N 2 13¾×20¼ in.
2 14×20¼ in. (not shown)

1×6—36 ft.

K 4 16 in.

L 8 20¾ in.
M 2 13¼ in.   **O** 2 16 in.
2 13½ in. (not shown)
1 32 in. (not shown)

1×2—1 ft.

Q 1 5¼ in.

1×1—6 ft.

P 2 16 in.
1 32 in. (not shown)

Glue, screws, 5d nails, plastic laminate and adhesive, twelve shelf supports, eight drawer guides, metal clips, four drawer pulls, 4-inch vinyl cove base, stain, and varnish.

STACKABLE STORAGE UNITS

Adding storage like this to an eating area is as easy as building a box—with the addition of a few custom features such as dividers and a drawer or two. All units are 15 inches deep, constructed of ¾-inch plywood and butt-joined to make cutting and assembling the components a hassle-free job. Display objets d'art or workaday items.

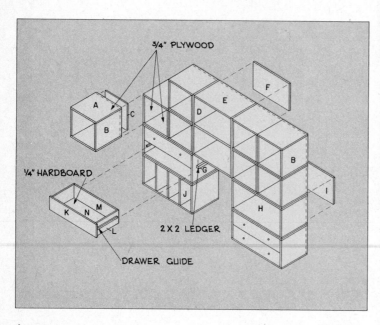

¾" PLYWOOD
¼" HARDBOARD
2 X 2 LEDGER
DRAWER GUIDE

1 Butt-join (see page 86) tops and bottoms (A) and sides (B) to form eight cubes (see sketch for joints). Use glue and nails throughout. Fit backs (C) into cubes. Glue and nail in place.

2 Butt-join sides (D) and horizontal pieces (E) of two center units, according to sketch. Insert back pieces (F) and glue and nail in place.

3 To construct four bottom units, assemble horizontals (H) and sides (B). Glue and nail backs (I) in place. Butt-join dividers (J) to top and bottom of one unit.

4 Cut ¼-in. dado (see page 87) in drawer sides (L) and backs (M) to receive bottoms (N). Construct drawers according to sketch, using glue and screws.

5 Install drawer guides. Fill holes, sand, finish. Add pulls.

6 Attach ledger (G) for tabletop.

Materials (for a grouping of units 60×84×15 inches deep):

¾-in. plywood—6½ shts.

A	16	15×15 in.
B	24	15×13½ in.
C	8	13½×13½ in.
D	2	30×15 in.
E	3	22½×15 in.
F	2	13⅞×22½ in.
H	8	30×15 in.
I	4	28½×13½ in.
J	3	14¼×13½ in.
K	4	6¾×28½ in.
L	8	6¾×13½ in.
M	4	6¾×25 in.

¼-in. hardboard—¾ sht.

N	4	25½×13 in.

2×2—2 ft. (optional)

G	2	10 in.

Glue, nails, screws, eight drawer guides and pulls, and paint.

PRACTICAL KITCHEN CAROUSEL

If there's a big vacant area in the center of your kitchen, put the space to use with a classy carousel like this one. It gives you four sets of adjustable shelves for a full floor-to-ceiling storage area you didn't have before. And it puts spices, dishes, and utensils just a spin away. This unit is skewered on a pipe anchored in flanges top and bottom.

1 Cut top and bottom hexagons (D) with 19-inch sides. Cut 3-inch hole in center for pipe. Cut 6x58-inch opening in uprights (G). Cut dadoes (see page 87) in verticals (G, L); install adjustable shelf supports as in sketch.

2 Miter (see page 88) inside edges of verticals (G) for 60-degree joint. Miter ends of trim (H, I). Screw and glue inside trim (H, I) and outer trim (J) in place.

3 Glue and screw two trimmed vertical panels (G) to each core piece (L) as shown. Butt-join (see page 86) vertical core pieces (K) to assemblies (G, L). Glue and screw.

4 Miter corners of nailers (F) and trim (E). Rabbet inside and kerf outside of nailers (F) as shown. Attach to underside of hexagons (D). Add trim (E).

5 Glue and screw hexagon assemblies to center section (G, L, K).

6 Weld metal supports (O) to pipe 12 inches above the floor. Grind ends of pipe flat. Lubricate with graphite. Thread pipe (C) through core of unit. Attach flange and baseplate (A) to floor. Place pipe in flanges. Plumb pipe and attach flange (B) to ceiling.

7 Cut shelves (M, N) to fit. Trim with vinyl edge veneer. Fill holes; sand and finish unit. Install shelves at desired heights.

Materials (for 40-inch-diameter unit 84 inches high):

3/4-in. plywood—4 shts.
- **D** 2 38-inch-diameter hexagon
- **G** 4 11½×64½ in.
- **K** 2 4×64½ in.
- **L** 2 8½×64½ in.
- **M** 8 15¾×15¾ in.
- **N** 8 29×14 in.

5/4×5/4—40 ft.
- **E** 12 20 in.
- **F** 12 19½ in.

½×¾—66 ft.
- **H** 8 58 in.
- **I** 8 6 in.
- **J** 4 64½ in.

Metal parts
- **A** 1 3-in. inside diameter flange and base plate
- **B** 1 3-in. inside diameter flange
- **C** 1 8-foot long 3-in. outside diameter pipe
- **O** 4 12 in. metal supports

Glue, screws, graphite, vinyl edge veneer, fourteen adjustable shelf supports, stain, and varnish.

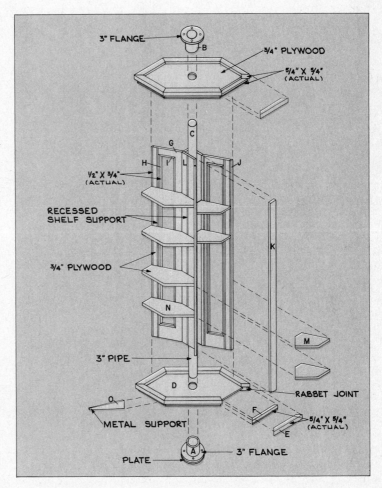

3" FLANGE
B
¾" PLYWOOD
5/4" X 5/4" (ACTUAL)
C
G
H I L J
½" X ¾" (ACTUAL)
RECESSED SHELF SUPPORT
¾" PLYWOOD
K
N
M
3" PIPE
D
O
METAL SUPPORT
RABBET JOINT
F
5/4" X 5/4" (ACTUAL)
E
PLATE
A
3" FLANGE

BUTCHER BLOCK/GLASS SHELVES

Put a whole wall to work as a storage and display area with this handsome shelf unit. It contrasts rugged butcher block and slim glass for shelves that look distinctive, yet don't cost a fortune to build. The butcher block is simply laminated 2x2 pine, and you can adjust the dimensions to fit your wall size, ceiling height, and the placement of your windows.

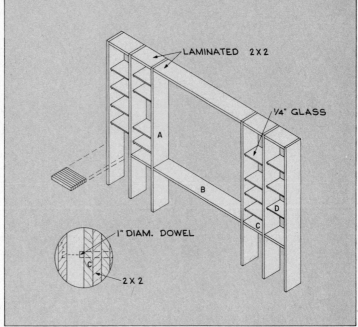

1 To construct laminated uprights (A), drill four holes in each 2x2 (see detail). Glue together with 1-inch dowels. Clamp until dry.
2 To construct shelves, drill four holes in each 2x2 of center shelf (B) and two holes in each 2x2 of side shelves (C). Glue together with dowels and clamp until dry.
3 Butt-join (see page 86) horizontal and vertical laminated sections (A, B, C) by drilling holes in both joining pieces and gluing together with 2- to 3-inch dowels. Clamp until dry.
4 Determine position of glass shelves (D). Drill holes in side sections (A) to accommodate the shelf brackets.

5 Sand and seal unit. Leave natural, or if desired, stain before finishing with at least two coats of varnish. Sand lightly and allow 24 hours drying time between coats.
6 Install brackets and shelves.

Materials (for a 12×8×1-ft. unit):

2×2—568 ft.
A 48 96 in.
B 16 71 in.
C 64 16 in.
1-in.-diameter dowels—52 ft.
   48 10½ in.
   40 2 to 3 in.
¼-in. tempered glass
D 15 15⅞×10½ in.
Glue, shelf brackets, sealer.

FLOOR-TO-CEILING CUPBOARD

Convert an opening or create one—either way, it's the first step to a contemporary "pantry" like the one shown here. Three easy-to-build units are attached to the sidewalls to form six shelves for storing dishes, glassware, and serving pieces. A pair of drawers hold silver, while the cubbyholes below accommodate place mats and napkins.

1 Frame support wall with 2x4 studs, single 2x4 plate at bottom, and double 2x4 plate at top, as shown in sketch.
2 Cover frame with plasterboard. Finish, paint, and trim with appropriate molding.
3 Construct three horizontal sections. Butt-join (see page 86) top and bottom (A) and sides (B) as shown in sketch. Use glue and screws. Glue and screw center divider (B) in place.
4 Screw completed sections into sidewalls.
5 Cut ¼-inch dado (see page 87) in drawer sides (D) and backs (E) to receive bottoms (F). Butt-join as shown in sketch.
6 Glue and screw bottoms (F) in place. Attach drawer fronts (C).
7 Install drawer guides on drawers and in top half of bottom section. Insert drawers.
8 Fill all holes and exposed plywood edges with wood putty. Sand well. If desired, use vinyl edge veneer to finish plywood edges. Prime unit, then paint at

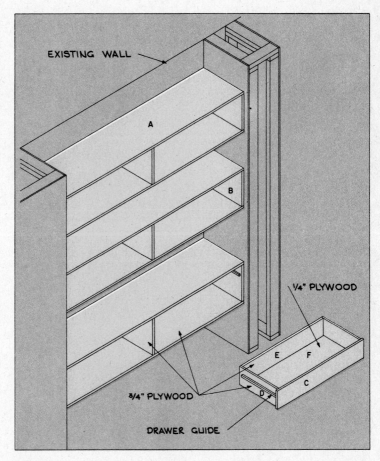

least two coats, sanding between. For a natural finish, use filler, stain, sealer, and varnish.

Materials (for shelf unit 72 inches wide and 16 inches deep):

A	6	72×16 in.
B	9	16×12 in.
C	2	34⅞×6 in.
D	4	6×15¼ in.
E	2	6×32⅜ in.

¼-in. plywood—½ sht.

F	2	32⅞×14¾ in.

Glue, screws, four drawer guides, and paint.

FANCY BUT FUNCTIONAL SHELVES

Back your breakfast table with a wall of shelves to store everything from spices and pans to cannisters and accessories. There's even a slanted book rack to display your favorite cookbooks. And, the whole unit is backed with warm wood paneling for a rustic look. Here's a way to increase shelf space and add to your kitchen decor all at the same time.

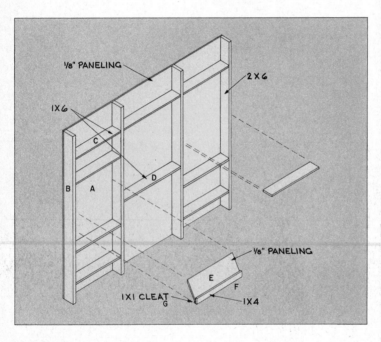

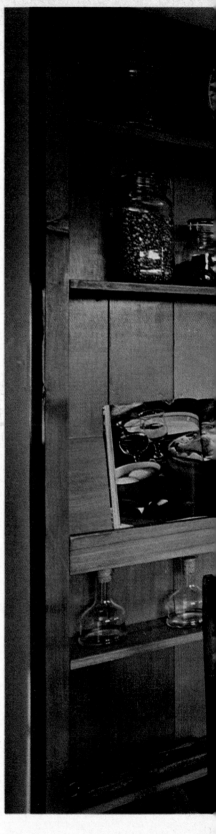

1 Butt-join (see page 86) vertical 1x6s (B) and shelves (C, D) as shown in sketch. Glue and nail shelves in place. (For more shelf strength, add ½ inch to length of shelves and cut ¼-inch dadoes or stopped dadoes in vertical members (B).)

2 Assemble slanted book rack (E, F, G) as shown in sketch. Miter (see page 88) top edge of E to fit against back (A). Flush front trim (F) with outer edge of verticals (B). Glue and nail in place.

3 Nail sections of back (A) in place as shown in sketch. Attach unit to wall by screwing into studs (see page 90).

4 Countersink nails and screws. Fill all holes with wood putty. Sand shelf unit well. Apply filler, then stain shelves and apply sealer. Finish with at least two coats of varnish, sanding lightly and allowing 24 hours drying time between coats.

Materials (for shelves to fit 8-foot-wide wall with 7-foot soffit height):

⅛-in. wood paneling—2¼ shts.
  A 2 48×84 in.
  E 1 12×27 in.
2×6—32 ft.
  B 4 84 in.
1×6—26 ft.
  C 8 27 in.   **D** 2 36 in.
1×4—4 ft.
  F 1 27 in.
1×1—4 ft.
  G 1 27 in.
Glue, nails, screws, filler, sealer, stain, and varnish.

ADJUSTABLE CORNER SHELVES

There's nothing complicated about the design of this sturdy shelf unit. It's made of 2x4 verticals, pegged with dowels to support 1x10 shelves. And it's constructed to give you plenty of shelf space on two adjacent walls. These shelves look great just the way they are—or if you prefer, stain or paint them. Then use them to store and show off your kitchen accessories.

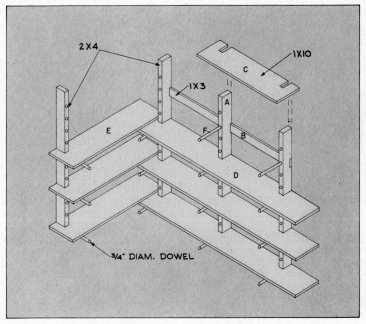

1 Drill eleven holes in each 2x4 (A) to receive dowels (F) as shown in sketch. Holes in 2x4 for left wall should be placed ¾-inch higher than holes in the right wall's verticals to keep overlapping shelves level.

2 Cut dadoes (see page 87) in back surfaces of right wall 2x4s (A) to receive 1x3s (B) as shown in sketch. Glue and screw 1x3 supports (B) in place.

3 Cut notches in shelves (C, D, E) to fit around 2x4s (A) as shown in sketch.

4 Attach assembled right wall section (A, B) to wall. Screw through 2x4s (A) into studs. Screw left side 2x4 to wall.

5 Place dowels in verticals (A) and position shelves (C, D, E) as shown in sketch.

6 Countersink screws and fill holes. Sand unit well. If desired, apply a filler, stain, and sealer before finishing with two coats of varnish.

Materials (for a corner unit 36×72×48 inches high):

2×4—16 ft.		
A	4	48 in.
1×3—10 ft.		
B	2	49½ in.
1×10—30 ft.		
C	1	32 in.
D	3	72 in.
E	3	36 in.
¾-in. dowels—14 ft.		
F	14	12 in.

Glue, screws, filler, sealer, stain, and varnish.

OVER-A-WINDOW SHELVES

1 Butt-join (see page 86) cross-members (B) and verticals (A) as shown in sketch. Use glue and nails.
2 Drill ½-inch holes every 2 inches in vertical supports.
3 Screw to window trim.
4 Insert dowels (C) in vertical supports (A). Add shelves (D).
5 Install cup hooks on cross-members (B) for hanging.
6 Paint or stain, if desired.

Materials (for 42×96×4¾ in. unit):

1×2—22 ft.
  A 2 96 in.   **B** 2 36 in.
½-in.-diameter dowels—3 ft.
  C 8 4 in.
⅜-in. tempered glass
  D 4 42×4 in.
Glue, nails, and cup hooks.

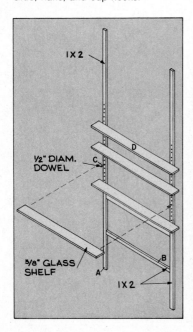

HANDY KITCHEN OFFICE

Add a few shelves and a desk top made from a solid core door, and you've turned the end of your kitchen cabinets into a mini-office. Shelves are adjustable to take care of any planning center supplies you have to store.

1 Cut dadoes (see page 87) in sides (A, B) and install adjustable shelf supports. Install shelf supports in bottom cabinet. Screw side (B) into studs of wall above base cabinet.

2 Cut radius corners on desk top (E). Cut rabbet (see page 87) in right side to fit around vertical (B). Cut dado in side (A) to receive desk top. Glue and screw desk top into base cabinet and side (A).

3 Install shelf brackets and shelves (C, D, F).

4 Countersink screws. Fill all holes and plywood edges with wood putty. Or use vinyl edge veneer on plywood edges.

5 Sand well. Apply primer and paint, or use filler, then stain. Apply sealer and finish with at least two coats of varnish. Allow 24 hours drying time between coats.

Materials (for a unit 43½ inches wide and 66 inches high):

¾-in. plywood—2 shts.

A	1	12×66 in.	**F**	2	12×28 in.
B	1	12×38 in.			
C	2	12×42 in.			
D	1	6×42 in.			

Solid-core door

E	1	43×24 in.

Glue, screws, six shelf supports, brackets, and paint or stain.

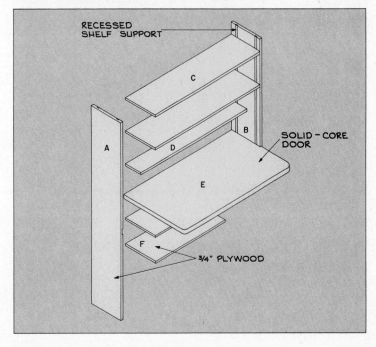

RECESSED SHELF SUPPORT

SOLID-CORE DOOR

¾" PLYWOOD

ELEGANT EATING AREAS

The most convenient place to eat is always in—or near—the kitchen. But sometimes that's easier said than done. Maybe your kitchen just doesn't have room for dining furniture—or perhaps you simply don't want to put the usual table and chairs in the usual place.

If your eating area needs problem-solving, space-saving, imaginative ideas, then this section is for you. Here are custom-designed snack counters, banquettes, mini-tables—and even island eating centers. And each one is planned to let you enjoy kitchen dining in short order.

Check over these projects to see how easily they can be adapted to fit exactly into whatever space you have. Measure your space carefully and decide how many people you'll want to accommodate. Then, using our materials lists as a starting point, make the necessary changes in dimensions. Finally, read through the building basics section at the back of the book. It will help brush up your carpentry techniques.

PENINSULA KITCHEN COUNTER

The end of a kitchen cabinet is just the beginning of a family dining area with a peninsula unit like this one. Vary its size and shape to fit your space and the number of diners. The laminated plastic top makes it a breeze to keep clean.

And with two roomy drawers for supplies, this tabletop also doubles as a kitchen desk and planning center.

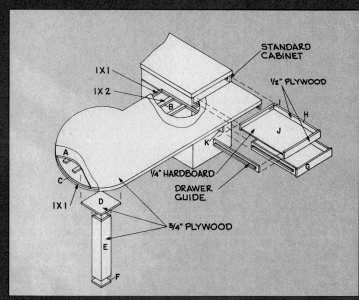

1 Cut tabletop (A) to desired shape and size. Glue and screw supports (B) to tabletop, 12-inches on center. Frame tabletop with 1x1 support (C) on edges, (to facilitate bending around curve, saw kerf the support (C) ⅓ the thickness of the 1x1). Glue and screw in place. Affix plastic laminate to top and edges.

2 Attach base (D) to underside. Miter edges (see page 88) of verticals (E); glue and screw together to form leg. Insert base (F) into bottom and attach.

3 Cut ¼-inch dado (see page 87) in drawer sides (H) and back (I) to receive bottom (J). Construct drawers (G, H, I, J) (see page 92).

4 Remove top part of cabinet end panel for drawer. Glue and screw tabletop to cabinet and wall. Attach drawer supports (K). Install drawer guides. Fill holes, sand, finish, and add drawer pulls.

Materials (for project shown):

$3/4$-in. plywood—1$1/2$ shts.

D	1	12×12 in.	**E**	4 27¾×5 in.
A	1	48×96 in. (shaped)		
F	1	3½×3½ in.		
K	2	23¼×3 in.		

$1/2$-in. plywood—¼ sht.

G	2	21×3 in.	**I**	2 19×3 in.
H	4	23¼×3 in.		

$1/4$-in. hardboard—¼ sht.

J 2 19½×23 in.

1×2—18 ft.

B 3 (cut to table size)

1×1—approx. 24 ft.

C 1 (cut to table size)

Four drawer guides, glue, screws, plastic laminate and adhesive, two drawer pulls, and stain.

BEAUTY OF A BANQUETTE

If a kitchen alcove is your permanent dining spot, it's a natural for a built-in banquette like this one. The table is made from a solid-core door with radius-cut corners, and is supported by cardboard concrete forms attached to the unit's raised floor. Make the benches as long as the platform, or extend them out into the kitchen.

1 Nail subfloor supports (D) to floor as shown in sketch. Rip 1x6 front riser (E) to 4¼ inches. Nail to front 2x4. Nail plywood floor (F) to supports.

2 Using glue and screws, butt-join (see page 86) vertical seat supports (G) and horizontal seat base supports (H) to form ten U-shaped units. Position as shown in sketch and attach to floor (F) using glue and screws.

3 Glue and screw seat pieces (I, J) to support units. Attach plywood (K, L) to front surface of seats. Use glue and screws to secure plywood to supports.

4 Miter corners (see page 88) of edgers (M, N) and attach as shown in sketch, using glue and screws. Attach plywood end panels (O).

5 Fill all holes and exposed plywood edges. Cut foam rubber cushions with mitered corners as shown in sketch. Cover with vinyl or fabric.

6 To construct table, cut door (A) to size and radius corners. Screw two plywood discs (C) into floor (F). Screw two discs in corresponding position on underside of top (A). Place forms (B) over floor discs. Rest table discs in top of forms. Screw through forms into discs. Paint or stain as desired.

Materials (for project shown):
U-shaped 4×8-foot seating unit:

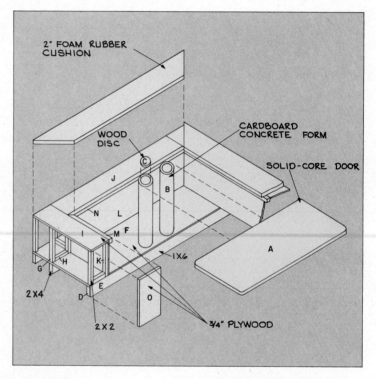

2×4—24 ft.
D 3 96 in.
1×6—8 ft.
E 1 96 in.
2×2—44 ft.
G 20 14 in.
H 10 9 in.
M 2 36 in.
N 1 72 in.
¾-in. plywood—3 shts.
F 1 48×96 in.
I 2 12¾×48 in.

J 1 12¾×70½ in.
K 2 14×36 in.
L 1 14×70½ in.
O 2 19×14¼ in.
For 30×60×30-inch-high table:
A 1 solid-core door
B 2 14-in.-diameter cardboard concrete forms 28 in. long
¾- in. plywood—½ sht.
C 4 13½-in.-diameter circles
Glue, screws, nails, 2-inch foam rubber, and paint or stain.

BREAKFAST BAR WITH STORAGE

Call it a snack counter, a serving center, or a dining table, this unit is a happy solution to three kitchen problems. It provides a butcher block top for family dining or an extra work surface and it gives always-welcome storage, too.

The under-the-table cabinet features doors that open on both sides for easy access to anything you tuck inside.

1 Form laminated top by drilling three holes in each 3x3 (A) to receive ½-inch dowels (R). Glue and clamp together all top pieces (A) and dowels. Radius corners.

2 Dado (see page 87) inside surfaces of sides (B) and divider (G) to receive shelf support standards. Butt-join (see page 86) top (D) and sides (B) as shown in sketch. Use glue and screws. Flush nailers (F) with bottom edge of side (B). Glue and screw in place. Attach bottom (C) to nailers (F). Glue and screw face board (I) in place.

3 Install vertical divider (G), using glue and screws. Attach shelf support standards. Insert shelves (H). Hinge doors (J) to cabinet (see page 93).

4 Butt-join top of support frame (K, M) using glue and screws. Join leg pieces (L, M) to top frame (M). With glue and screws, attach cabinet to 2x4 frame, screwing through sidewalls of cabinet to 2x4s.

5 Place nailers (Q) between joists under the floor deck corresponding with the placement of the finished unit. Bolt through the leg (M), floor, and nailer (Q).

6 Miter (see page 88) joining edges of facing pieces (N, O, P). With glue and screws, attach facing pieces (E, N, O, P) to 2x4 frame. Glue laminated top (A) to unit.

7 Countersink screws and fill all holes with wood putty. Fill edges of exposed plywood or use edging tape. Sand the unit well. To paint, use primer and at least two coats of paint with light

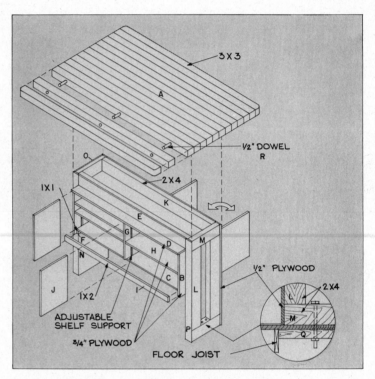

sanding between coats. For a natural wood finish, use a filler (see page 96), then stain. Seal the stain before finishing with varnish. Use at least two top coats with a minimum of 24 hours drying time and light sanding between coats. Rub down with steel wool and wax.

Materials (for a unit 54×35×36-inches high):

3×3 fir—70 ft.
A	14	54 in.

½-in. dowel—10 ft.
R	3	33 in.

¾-in. plywood—2½ shts.
B	2	14½×17½ in.
C	1	16×38½ in.
D	1	19×40 in.
E	2	3½×40 in.
G	1	13×17½ in.
H	3	17½×18⅞ in.
J	8	10×14½ in.

1×1—4 ft.   1×2—8 ft.
F	2	16 in.
I	2	38½ in.

2×4—22 ft.
K	2	40 in.
L	4	26½ in.
M	4	11 in.
Q	2	12 in.

½-in. plywood—½ sht.
N	2	12×14¾ in.
O	2	12×33½ in.
P	4	3½×33½ in.

Eight adjustable shelf supports, sixteen flush door hinges, four touch latches, glue, screws, 8-inch bolts with nuts, washers, paint or stain.

KING-SIZE SEATING FOR A KITCHEN

If your kitchen eating area is the gathering spot for everything from neighborhood coffees to family conferences, this is the unit to solve your seating problems. It's a generous L-shaped bench with 5 feet of cushioned comfort on each side. And though it looks built-in, it's actually portable. Move it easily from one corner to another—wherever you want practical seating.

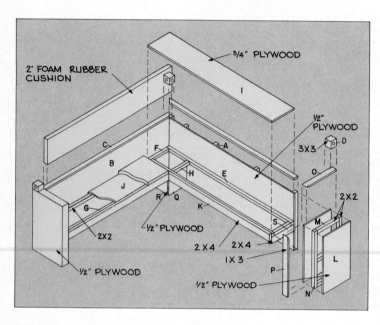

1 With glue and screws, attach 2x2s (A) flush with backs (B). Miter (page 88) back pieces (B).
2 Secure 2x4 ledgers (S) to each end of seat back unit as shown in sketch. Butt-join (see page 86) ledgers (E, F, G, H). Glue and screw.
3 Butt-join corner box support pieces (Q, R), using glue and screws. Secure box to plywood back pieces (B). Attach assembled ledgers (E, F, G, H) to box, 2x4s (S), and backs (B).
4 Butt-join ends of trim (K) and attach to 2x4s (S) and ledger unit. Glue and screw on seats (I, J). Miter and attach trim (C).
5 Butt-join frame pieces (M, N). Miter facing (P, O). Attach facing (P, O, L) to frame (M, N). Drill 1½-inch holes in blocks (D). Attach. Cover with plastic laminate, or paint. Add cushions.

Materials (for unit 80×80×28¾ inches high):

2×2—74 ft.					
A,N	14	28 in.	**E**	1	75 in.
F	2	73½ in.	**G**	1	60 in.
H	3	12 in.	**M**	6	14¾ in.

1×3—22 ft.					
C	2	77½ in.	**P**	2	28¾ in.
O	2	18½ in.			

3×3—1 ft.		
D	3	2½ in.

2×4—14 ft.					
K	2	60 in.	**S**	2	15 in.

½-in. plywood—2 shts.					
Q	2	12×14 in.	**R**	2	12×13 in.
B	2	28×75½ in.			
L	4	17¾×28 in.			

¾-in. plywood—1 sht.					
I	1	15×75 in.	**J**	1	15×60 in.

Glue, screws, 2-inch foam rubber, and semi-gloss enamel.

SNACK BAR CABINET

A tall, slender storage cabinet is a nice addition to your kitchen just the way it is, but add a detachable snack bar and you've really added convenience. This unit features a top and bottom cabinet, plus a pair of open shelves. And when the table's not in service, remove the leg, slide out the top, and stash it in a closet or cabinet until you need it.

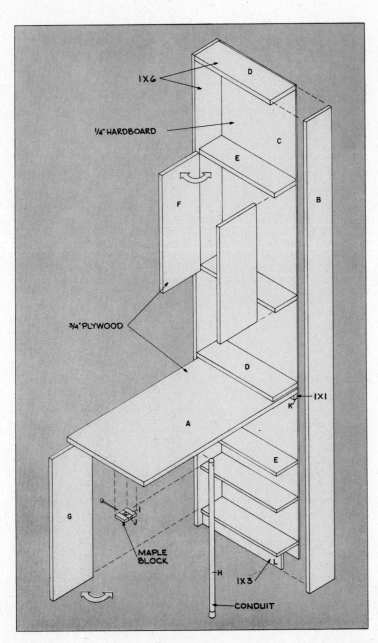

1 Butt-join (see page 86) sides (B) and top (D), using glue and screws. Flush fronts of sides and top. Attach back (C).
2 Attach shelf support (L) and shelves (D, E) as shown in sketch. Install ledger (K) 1-inch below shelf (D). Hinge doors (F, G) (see page 93). Install latches.
3 Glue plastic laminate to table-top (A). Drill holes in leg (H) and in blocks (J) to receive bolt. With glue and screws, attach leg brace (I, J) to underside of table as shown in sketch. Bolt on leg (H) and add rubber tip.
4 Fill holes; sand well; paint. Add door trim if desired.

Materials (for an 84×18×5½-inch-deep unit):

1×6—26 ft.
B 2 84 in.
D 2 16½ in.
     (milled to 5¼ in.)
E 5 16½ in.
     (milled to 4½ in.)
1×1—2 ft.
K 1 16½ in.
1×3—2 ft.
L 1 16½ in.
¾-in. plywood—½ sht.
A 1 16½×30 in.
F 2 8¼×21 in.
G 2 8¼×25 in.
¼-in. hardboard—½ sht.
C 1 16½×84 in.
¾-in. conduit
H 1 29 in.
Maple blocks—cut to size
I 2 ¾×2×½ in.
J 2 ¾×¾×½ in.
One ¼-inch bolt 3½ inches long, eight butt hinges, glue, screws, plastic laminate and adhesive, latches, rubber tip, and paint.

PIPE-LEGGED KITCHEN TABLE

Pipe dreams *are* practical—when they turn into realities like this elegant rollaway table. The underpinning is made of ¾-inch pipe and fittings—a simple, inexpensive way to support any tabletop. Here, they serve as legs for a laminated hardwood top with radius corners. But if you prefer, make your tabletop of plywood and apply laminated plastic.

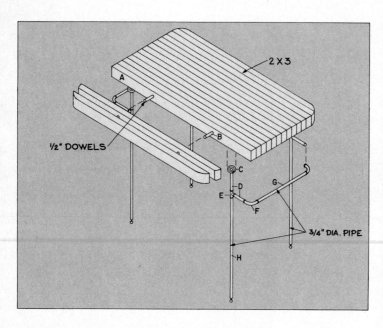

2 X 3

½" DOWELS

3/4" DIA. PIPE

1 Drill two holes in each 2x3 (A) to receive ½-inch dowels (B) as shown in sketch. With wood glue, assemble all hardwood strips and dowels. Clamp together firmly and let dry. Radius corners. Sand.

2 Screw elbows (F) to towel bars (G). Screw side pieces (D) to elbows (F). Add tees (E) to ends of assembled towel bars.

3 Screw legs (H) into bottom of each connector (E). Screw top pipe sections (D) into top of each connector (E). Add floor flanges (C) to top of each leg.

4 Screw floor flanges (C) to underside of laminated tabletop.

Add ball casters to the bottom of each leg (H).

Materials (for a 24×54×30-in.-high table):

2×3 maple—80 ft.
  A 16 54 in.
¹/₂-in. dowels—6 ft.
  B 2 23 in.
³/₄-in. pipe—16 ft.
  D 8 6 in.   **H** 4 19 in.
  G 2 18 in.
³/₄-in. fittings
  C 4 floor flanges
  E 4 tees
  F 4 90-degree elbows
Glue, screws, and four 1-inch diameter ball casters.

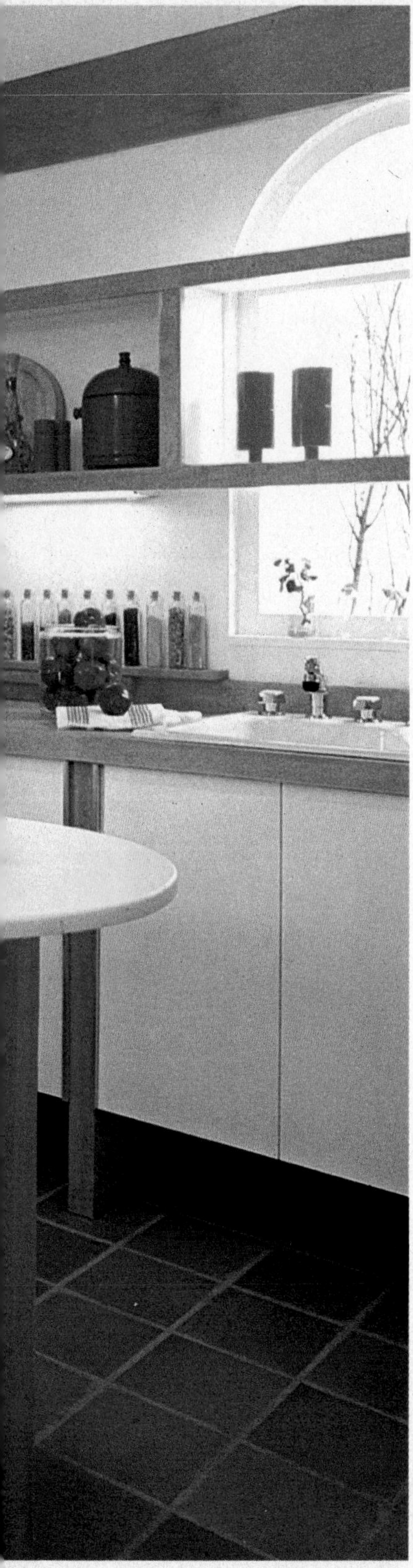

MULTIPURPOSE KITCHEN COUNTER

Add a snack counter like this one and you've turned an L-shaped kitchen into a U-shape. You've also added more storage space, more work surface, and a convenient eating area.

This versatile unit is designed to provide knee space for snackers and still give you a handy cabinet for cookware or small appliances on the "business side".

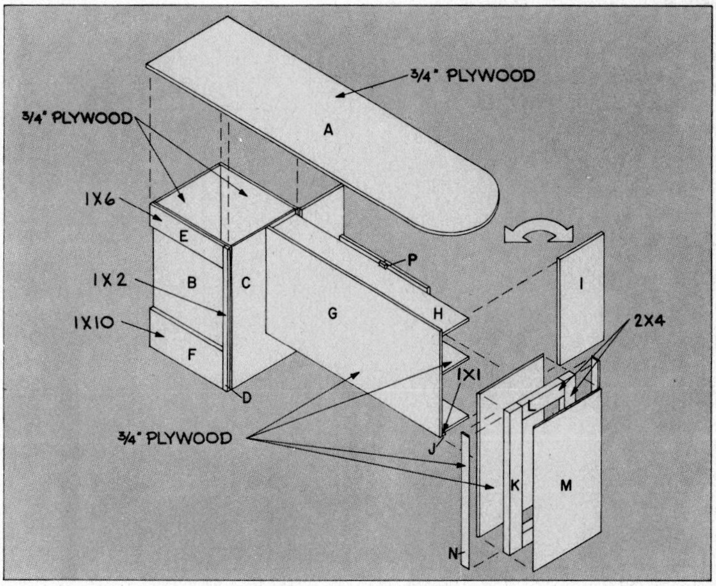

1 Butt-join (see page 86) box sides (B, C) as shown in sketch. Use glue and screws. Add trim pieces (D, E, F).
2 Butt-join end support frame (L, K). Miter (see page 88) edges of facing pieces (N, M). Attach.
3 Notch the shelves (H). Following sketch, assemble center cabinet (H, G, J, P). Attach to end units. Add 25¾-inch 1x2 as center hinge strip. Hinge doors (I) (see page 93). Install door latches.
4 Cut 1-foot radius on one end of tabletop (A). Glue plastic laminate to top and sides. Glue top to base unit.
5 Countersink screws. Fill holes with wood putty. Use a primer, then paint at least two coats of satin finish enamel. Sand lightly between coats.

Materials (24×90×36-in. unit):

3/4-in. plywood—2 1/2 shts.
A 1 24×90 in.
B 2 21½×35¼ in.
C 2 20¾×35¼ in.
G 1 25¾×52½ in.
H 3 10×52½ in.
I 4 13 1/16×25¾ in.
M 2 22¼×35¼ in.
N 2 3×35¼ in.
1×2—6 ft.
D 1 35¼ in. **P** 1 25¾ in.
1×6—2 ft.
E 1 20 in.
1×10—2 ft.
F 1 20 in.
1×1—6 ft.
J 1 52½ in.
2×4—10 ft.
K 2 35¼ in. **L** 2 13¾ in.
Glue, screws, plastic laminate and adhesive, eight pivot hinges, door latches, and paint.

KITCHEN CORNER CAFE

Kitchen meals are like eating at your favorite cafe when your dining spot features a cozy booth like this one.

The natural-finish planks and sparkling white wood and laminate combine to give this unit a contemporary flavor. But don't let that stop you traditionalists. Change the color and the surroundings—and this trio fits anywhere.

1 Miter (see page 88) corners of table frame (A, B). Glue and screw frame and tabletop (C) together. Use adhesive to affix plastic laminate to tabletop and edges.

2 Following sketch, glue and screw nailer (G) to ledger (F) with top edges flush. Glue and screw table support (E) to nailer (G). Table frame (A) will rest on ledger (F) between the ends of support (E) and the wall.

3 Cut detail in table leg (D) as shown in sketch. Butt-join (see page 86) leg (D) and support (E).

4 Screw table base (D, E, F, G) to wall through ledger (F). Place tabletop on base. Secure with glue and screws through support board (E) into underside of plywood tabletop (C).

5 For seats, glue two layers of legs (H) together to form four 1-inch-thick leg pieces. Cut leg details as shown in sketch. At the bottom of seat backs (N), cut 1 × 18½-inch notch on each end. Glue and screw backs (N) to legs (H). Cut details in braces (I) and butt-join to legs (H) as shown in sketch so that top edges are flush.

6 Cut shims (M) to the angle desired for pitch of seat back. Glue and screw to back (N).

7 Position the 5/4-inch boards (J, L, K) as shown in the sketch. Use glue and screws to fasten. Countersink the screws on 5/4-inch boards and fill with wood plugs.

8 Countersink all screws. Fill holes and exposed plywood edges with wood putty. Use sanding sealer on all plywood surfaces for a smooth finish.

9 Paint seat backs, legs, and braces. Use at least two coats of semi-gloss enamel.

10 For natural finish parts of the unit, prepare surfaces (see page 96) and use at least two coats of clear varnish.

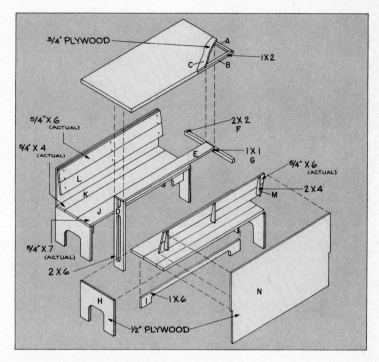

Materials (for project shown):

For 30×60×30-in.-high table:
1×2—16 ft.
- **A** 2 30 in.   **B** 2 60 in.

3/4-in. plywood—1 sht.
- **C** 1 30×60 in.

2×6—6 ft.
- **E** 1 55½ in.   **D** 1 27¾ in.

2×2—4 ft.
- **F** 1 27 in.

1×1—1 ft.
- **G** 1 5½ in.

For 60-in.-wide seats:
½-in. plywood—3 shts.
- **H** 8 15½×18½ in.
- **N** 2 60×36 in.

1×6—10 ft.
- **I** 2 58 in.

2×4—6 ft.
- **M** 6 9 in.

5/4×6—20 ft.
- **L** 4 60 in.

5/4×4—10 ft.
- **K** 2 60 in.

5/4×7—20 ft.
- **J** 4 60 in.

Screws, glue, plastic laminate and adhesive, wood plugs, sanding sealer, paint, and varnish.

PROJECTS FOR MORE LIVABLE KITCHENS

A woman spends more time in the kitchen than in any other room of the house! And the rest of the family isn't far behind in hours spent around the kitchen table or raiding the refrigerator. So for those reasons, anything that can be added to the kitchen or surrounding areas to make them more livable is a good investment indeed.

Here's a selection of ideas for your kitchen that will do just that. You'll find handy organizers, good-looking light fixtures, space-saving storage shelves—even a sink cabinet caddy.

Each one of these projects is easy to build, relatively inexpensive, and comes complete with a materials list and how-to instructions. In some cases you'll want to alter the measurements to fit your particular area or needs. Or you may want to adapt the designs to fit your kitchen decor. All these ideas can be customized to fit your life-style.

When your kitchen has all the essentials you need, it's time to think about adding these extra special "extras".

BURLAP-BACKED CATCHALL

Store-bought spice racks are expensive—and they're never exactly the size and shape you need for your kitchen. So the solution to the problem is to build a unit like this one. It's not only a well-organized spice rack, but it features an area for hanging flatware and a row of cuphooks to suspend everything from your kitchen shears and measuring spoons to whisks and strainers.

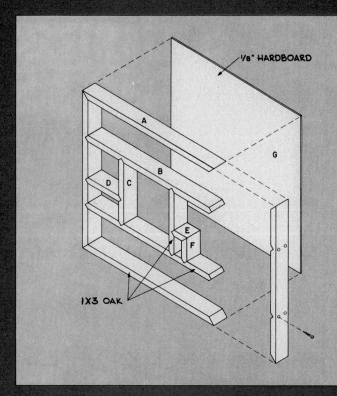

1 Miter (see page 88) corners of frame pieces (A). Cut Vs in side frame pieces (A) to accommodate horizontals (B, D) as shown in sketch. Glue and screw frame pieces together.

2 Cut Vs in other members (B, C) to receive interior dividers (C, D, E, F). Cut double miters on joining pieces (B, C, D, E, F) as shown in sketch. Glue and screw all pieces together.

3 Glue burlap on back (G). Glue and screw back (B) to frame.

4 Drill holes in back (G) for flatware hanging bolts. Screw nuts part way onto bolts. Insert bolts through holes in back (G). Screw second set of nuts on bolts to lock in place.

5 Screw cuphooks to bottom of frame.

Materials (for a 26×26×2⅝-in. unit):

1×3 oak—16 ft.

A	4 26 in.	B	2 25 in.
C	2 11 in.	D	1 7 in.
E	1 3 in.	F	1 4½ in.

⅛-in. hardboard—½ sht.

G	1 26×26 in.

Screws, glue, burlap, ten brass bolts, twenty nuts, and fifteen cuphooks.

PULL-DOWN SINK CADDY

The best place to keep sponges, pot scrapers, and dishwashing aids used to be under the sink. But not anymore! Now the most practical spot for these items is in this clever little pull-down caddy tucked into the wasted space of the top panel of the sink cabinet. Twin compartments attached to the back of the panel keep necessities within easy reach.

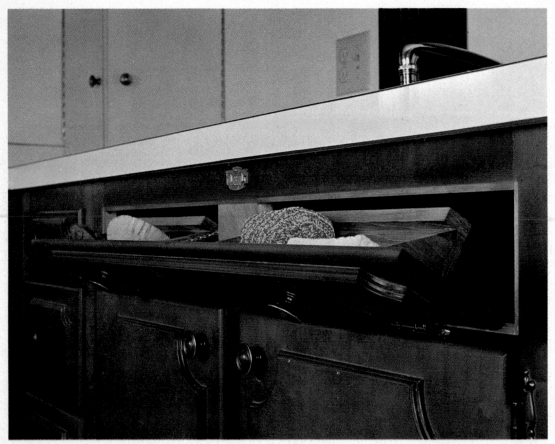

1 Remove cabinet top panel.
2 Cut sides (B) to slope from 3 inches to 1 inch at back edge. Glue and nail sides (B) to bottoms (A) as shown in sketch.
3 Glue and nail on backs (C).
4 Glue and nail assembled unit to back side of cabinet panel. Countersink nails. Fill holes.
5 Coat compartments with polyurethane varnish.
6 Hinge (see page 93) panel to cabinet. Install door pulls.

Materials (for a unit to fit a 36-in.-wide sink cabinet):
1×3—4 ft.
  A 2 16 in.
1×2—4 ft.
  C 2 16 in.
½-in. plywood
  B 4 3×2½ in.
Nails, glue, two door hinges, two door pulls, and varnish.

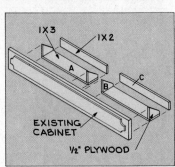

1X3
1X2
A
B
C
EXISTING CABINET
½" PLYWOOD

WALL-HUNG TELEPHONE CENTER

Surround your wall-hung kitchen phone with all the conveniences that make phoning a snap. This well-designed organizer provides a place for the phone book, a surface for pinning up messages, plus a cubbyhole and drawer for everything from paper and pencils to extra keys. This easy-to-build unit instantly improves any little section of wall space around your kitchen telephone.

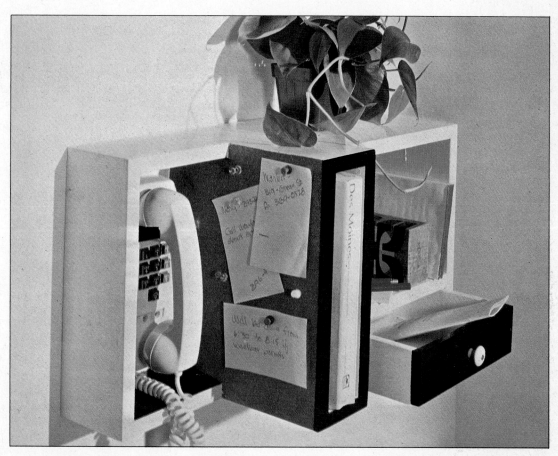

1 Cut top and bottom (A) to shape shown in sketch. Miter (see page 88) all edges shown in sketch.

2 Notch dividers (H) to receive top and bottom (A).

3 With glue and screws, assemble frame (A, B, C). Add dividers (H) and shelf (D).

4 Construct drawer (E, F, G) (see page 92). Finish. Add drawer pull.

Materials (20×13×9½-in. unit):

1×10—4 ft.   1×4—2 ft.
  A 2 20 in.   **B** 1 13 in.
1×3—4 ft.
  E 1 11¼ in.   **F** 2 4¾ in.
  I 1 9¾ in.
1×6—4 ft.
  C 1 13 in.   **D** 1 11¼ in.
½-in. plywood—¼ sheet
  G 1 4¼×10¼ in.
  H 2 13×9½ in.
Glue, screws, drawer pull, paint.

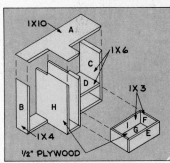

1X10   A   1X6   C   D   1X3   B   H   F   I   G   E   1X4   ½" PLYWOOD

CIRCLE
LATH
LAMP

If you still think of lath only as the perfect material for a trellis, this project will be a pleasant surprise.

1 Cut out center of circles (A) to form 13-inch diameter openings.
2 Glue and nail 16 lath strips (B) on inside of circles (A).
3 Drill hole in middle of disc (C). Wire sockets to underside of disc (C).

4 Glue and nail 16 strips (B) around outside of circle (A).

Materials (for a 16-in.-dia., 10-in.-high lamp):

½-in. plywood—¼ sht.
  A 2 16-in.-dia. circles
  C 1 12½-in.-dia. circle
1½ × ¼-in. lath—28 ft.
  B 32 10 in.
Glue, nails, four porcelain sockets, and electrical cord.

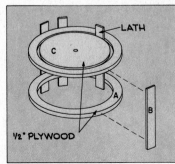

TIC-TAC-TOE CEILING FIXTURE

The simple geometry of this lamp is what makes it such a winner. The major elements of this ceiling-mounted "tic-tac-toe" design are made of 2x10s for a hefty, natural look.

In this case, four frosted globes finish the unit and give it a classic contemporary flavor. If your home would be brightened by a good-looking light—try this one.

1 Cut a notch 4 inches in from the end of each crosspiece (A) to allow members to interlock as shown in sketch. Drill holes for fixture cords in center of sides as shown.

2 Glue and screw together main elements (A); countersink screws.

3 Drill holes in top and bottom (B) to provide for mounting. Glue and screw in place. Flush top with crosspieces (A). Recess bottom (B) 1 inch.

4 Stain. Mount sockets or lamps to sides of light fixture.

Materials (for an 18×18×9½-in. lamp):

2×10—6 ft.
  A 4 18 in.
½-in. plywood—¼ sht.
  B 2 7×7 in.
Glue, nails, four sockets, cord, lamp fittings, and stain.

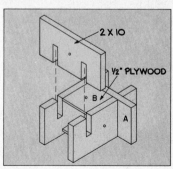

MINI-STORAGE SHELF UNIT

This see-through shelf unit does a big job in your kitchen without looking heavy and massive. The handsome butcher block shelves are made by laminating strips of ½-inch plywood. And acrylic sheet sides let you see what's being stored while giving the whole unit a light, airy look. Here's a kitchen helper you'll really enjoy.

1 Form top, bottom, and shelf (B) by laminating plywood strips. Use 23 strips for each section. Apply glue to surfaces, clamp together, and let dry completely. (NOTE: Resin glue is most effective for this type lamination.)

2 Cut (or have cut) acrylic sheet to proper size. Before removing protective paper covering, drill holes to accommodate screws.

3 Sand laminated sections well. Coat with polyurethane varnish to make wood impervious to moisture or spills.

4 Position sides (A), top, bottom, and shelf (B) and join with screws.

Materials (for a 12×12×30-in. unit):

½-in. plywood—¾ sht.
  A 69 1¾×12 in.
¼-in. acrylic sheet
  B 2 12×30 in.
Glue, screws, and polyurethane.

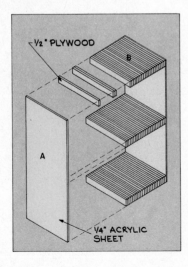

END-OF-THE-CABINET SHELVES

In a lot of kitchens, the range is situated at the end of a bank of kitchen cupboards, leaving a flat and very usable vertical surface near the cooktop. Here that surface has been put to good use with a cabinet-mounted mini-shelf. It's easy to build, adds a touch of color to an all-wood kitchen, and puts spices or condiments where you need them most.

1 Butt-join (see page 86) front surface (C) to bottom shelf (D). Use glue and screws.

2 Butt-join back (A) to bottom shelf (D) as shown in sketch. Use glue and screws.

3 Butt-join front (C) to top shelf (B). With glue and screws attach shelf (B) to back (A).

4 Fill all holes with wood putty. Sand well. Apply primer and paint unit two coats, sanding lightly between coats.

5 Screw unit into end of existing cabinet. Countersink screws, fill holes, and touch up paint. Or attach unit to wall (see page 90 for fastening methods).

Materials (for an 11½×18-in. unit):

1×12—4 ft.

A	1	17¼ in.
B	1	milled to 4½ in.
C	2	milled to 2½ in.
D	1	milled to 5¼ in.

Glue, screws, primer, paint.

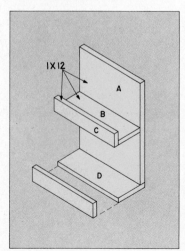

STAINED GLASS FIXTURE

The beauty of a stained glass panel doesn't have to be limited to windows. Here's one put to work as a light fixture. This design adapts easily to any size panel, with the window simply resting on the bottom flange of the frame. We've given you instructions to make the fixture of wood, but if you're handy with plastic, give it a try as framing material.

1 Miter (see page 88) sides (B, C) and lip (D, E). Attach lip to frame. Attach top (A). Use glue and nails. Countersink nails.
2 Finish. Attach fixtures.

Materials (for a 25½×13½× 7½-in. fixture):

½ in. plywood—¼ sheet
  A 1 12×24 in.
1×8—8 ft.
  B 2 25½ in.   **C** 2 13½ in.
1×1—6 ft.
  D 2 24 in.
Framed stained glass panel
  E 1 12×24 in.
Glue, nails, paint or stain, and two fluorescent fixtures.

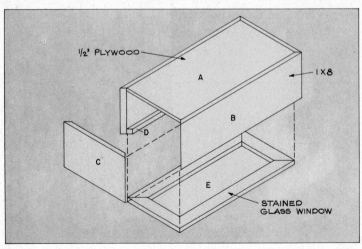

½" PLYWOOD — A
1×8
B
C
D
E
STAINED GLASS WINDOW

ALUMINUM SHADED LIGHT

This chain-hung ceiling fixture contrasts the grain of natural wood cross beams with the slick surface of sheet aluminum shades. Though this designer light looks like it cost a bundle to have custom-made—it's really inexpensive when you build it yourself. So why settle for a run-of-the-mill light when this kind of class is within easy reach?

1 Cut notches in center of two crosspieces (A) as shown in sketch. Cut notches in ends of crosspieces (A) to accommodate light fixtures. Stain as desired.

2 Screw light sockets to ends of crosspieces (A).

3 Bend aluminum to produce a 4-inch-diameter shade with a 1-inch flange on each end.

4 Screw through flange into 2x6s (A) to secure shades.

5 Screw eyebolts to top of crosspieces (A) as shown in sketch. Attach chain to eyebolts. Thread light cord through chain.

6 Join chain and cord to ceiling plate.

Materials (for 18×18-in. unit):

2×6—4 ft.
  A 2 17 in.
22-gauge aluminum—cut to size
  B 4 5½×16 in.
Screws, eye bolts, four light sockets, wire, chain, ceiling plate, and stain.

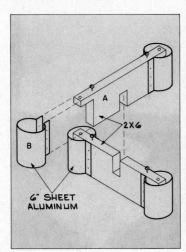

TILE COUNTER-SAVER

These four tiles, inset in your kitchen countertop, can become the most attractive trivet you've ever owned. And there's no searching around for it when you need it. Simply make a cut in your countertop, follow the instructions below, and create your own permanent countertop-saver. Use terra-cotta or glazed ceramic tile to blend with your counter or choose a sparkling accent color for kitchen contrast.

1 Cut a 12x12-inch square in the countertop.
2 Face with plywood (A), glued and screwed in place from the underside of the countertop.
3 Apply sealer to wood.
4 Apply mastic to the plywood (A) to secure tiles (B) within countertop opening.
5 Grout the tiles in place to finish the edges and seal cracks.

Materials (for a 12×12-in. insert):

¹/₂-in. plywood—¹/₄ sht.
  A 1 14×14 in.
Terra-cotta or glazed tile
  B 4 6×6-in. tiles
Glue, screws, wood sealer, mastic, and tile grout.

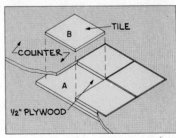

TILE
COUNTER
B
A
¹/₂" PLYWOOD

KNIFE RACK CUTTING BOARD

There's nothing handier than a countertop cutting board, unless it's a cutting board with its own built-in knife rack. Here's a kitchen addition that makes chopping, slicing, or carving a snap. Build the cutting board by laminating hardwood strips, then fashion the knife rack by routing out the hardwood board that rests on the backsplash.

1 Drill two holes in each 1½×1½ (A) to accommodate dowels (B). Glue, insert dowels, and clamp together until dry. Sand.

2 Rout various-width slots in backboard (D).

3 Glue and screw together knife rack pieces (C, D). Glue and screw to cutting board as shown.

Materials (for a 21×24¾-in. cutting board):

1½×1½ hardwood—28 ft.
  A 14 23¼ in.
½-in. dowel—4 ft.
  B 2 19½ in.
¾×5 hardwood—4 ft.
  C 1 21 in.
  D 1 21 in. (milled to 2 in.)
Glue and screws.

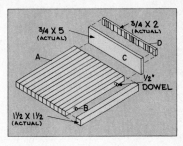

ALL-PURPOSE WALL UNIT

A telephone, a bulletin board, a note pad, and a pencil rack are all incorporated in this trim and efficient kitchen wall unit. You can even hang a mirror on the bulletin board for last min- ute touch-ups before answer- ing the door bell. And all it takes to put this addition to work in your kitchen is a sim- ple plywood-backed frame and a small section of cork.

1 Miter (see page 88) the ends of the top and bottom (A) and the sides (B).
2 Join frame pieces (A, B) with glue and screws. Screw back (C) to assembled frame.
3 Glue and screw dividers (D) in place. Screw to wall through back (C). Glue dividers (F) in place against back. Screw and glue on front (E) as shown.
4 Fill all holes and edges. Sand the unit well. Apply stain and at least two coats of varnish. (see page 96).
5 Glue on cork (G). Install door pull for phone cord.

Materials (for 18×48-in. unit):

1×3—12 ft.
  A 2 48 in.
  E 1 8¼ in.
  B 2 18 in.
1×2—4 ft.
  D 2 16½ in.
¼-in. plywood—¼ sht.
  C 1 17½×47½ in.
  F 3 ¾×2½ in.
¼-in. cork
  G 1 16½×28½ in.
Glue, screws, adhesive, one door pull, stain, and varnish.

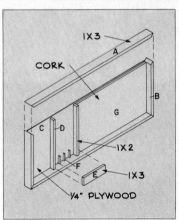

NATURAL REDWOOD LAMP

If the chalet look is what you're after for your kitchen/dining area, nothing will give it to you faster than this massive redwood light fixture. It's easy to build with "light boxes" attached to the ends of heavy crossbeams. A beveled-edge block finishes the bottom of the fixture and the whole unit hangs solidly from a length of rugged metal chain.

1 Cut dadoes (see page 87) in top of crosspieces (A) for cord. Lap-join (see page 86) crosspieces (A) as shown.
2 Miter edges of side pieces (B). Glue and screw together.
3 Drill holes; attach sockets to sides (B). Glue and screw assembled sides (B) to crosspieces (A).
4 Cut ¼-inch rabbet (see page 87) in bottom frame pieces (C, D); butt-join all frames (see page 86).
5 Insert glass (E) into bottom frames. Attach bottom frames to sides. Attach top frames. Bevel block (F) and attach.

Materials (for a 46×46-in. fixture):

4×6—6 ft.
 A 2 30 in.
 F 1 3×5½×5½-in. block
1×8—16 ft.
 B 16 12 in.
1×2—16 ft.
 C 16 8 in.　　　　**D** 16 5 in.
¼-in. frosted glass
 E 4 5½×5½ in.
Glue, screws, four double sockets, cord, and chain.

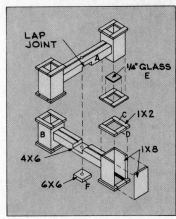

LAP JOINT

¼" GLASS E

C 1X2

D

1X8

4X6

B

6X6 F

A

STAIRSTEP SPICE RACK

A tri-level rack like this one puts a little spice in your kitchen decor—and it keeps your spices organized and close-at-hand. Place the unit on your countertop or hang it on a wall close to your cook center. In either place, it's a great way to beat the high cost of fancy racks and containers. Make your rack to fit whatever size jars or spice cans you have.

1 Cut end pieces (A) as shown in sketch.

2 Butt-join (see page 86) ends (A) and back (C) as shown.

3 Position shelves (B) as shown. Glue and screw to assembled ends and back (A, C).

4 Glue and screw railing pieces (D) in place as shown in sketch.

5 Countersink screws. Fill all holes with wood putty. Fill exposed plywood edges or finish with veneer tape.

6 Sand unit well. Prime and paint or stain and varnish.

Materials (for a 15×10×10½-in. unit):

½-in. plywood—½ sht.
A 2 8½×9 in.
B 3 14×3 in.
C 1 15×10½ in.
Screen bead—8 ft.
D 6 15 in.
Glue, screws, veneer tape, wood putty, and stain or paint.

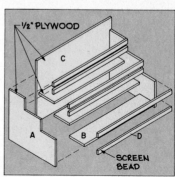

½" PLYWOOD
C
A
B
D
SCREEN BEAD

KITCHEN PROJECT BASICS

At some stage of your project, chances are you're going to need a little help. Maybe you'll need to know how to make a lap joint . . . how to hang your project on a wall . . . or how to build a drawer.

Well, look no further! The answers to these and many other frequently asked questions are presented clearly and concisely in this section.

Whether it's an organizer, work center, eating area, or shelving unit you're tackling, this section will help you do it better, more quickly, and with less effort.

COMMON CONSTRUCTION MATERIALS

The materials you use for construction will vary, depending on the item's intended use. So when making your selection, ask yourself these questions: Are you constructing something for indoor or outdoor use? Is the item strictly utilitarian, or will it be suitable for use in a living room? Is it intended for light-duty use, or will it be a long-lived project subject to considerable use—and abuse?

Hardboard

Hardboard is available in 4x8-foot sheets and comes in ⅛- and ¼-inch thicknesses. Standard hardboard is an excellent choice for cabinetwork, drawer bottoms, and concealed panels.

You can also get hardboard perforated with holes spaced about one inch apart. Perforated hardboard is recommended for building storage for soiled laundry and for the backs of hi-fi cabinets. The quarter- and eighth-inch perforated hardboard lends itself to storing garden equipment and tools, too, as its holes accept hooks designed for this purpose. To expand or change the arrangement, just switch the hooks around. If the project will be subject to dampness, use tempered hardboard.

Particle board, chip board, and flake board, also members of the hardboard family, have a coarser grain structure, are lighter in color, and are available in thicknesses up to ¾ inch. These products are made of granulated or shredded wood particles forced together under pressure with a binder at high temperatures.

Plywood

Plywood also comes in 4x8-foot sheets, though larger sheets are available on special order. Thicknesses range from ⅛-inch to ¾-inch. For light-duty storage, the ¼- and ½-inch thicknesses are adequate. If you are planning to build an outdoor storage unit, specify *exterior grade* when making your purchase. Exterior grade plywood has its layers glued together with a waterproof glue to withstand rain.

The surfaces of plywood sheets are graded A, B, C, and D—with A the smoother, better surface and D the least desirable appearance. Choose AA (top grade, both sides) only for projects where both sides will be exposed; use a less expensive combination for others.

Solid Wood

Plain, ordinary wood still ranks as the most popular building material. Wood is sold by the "board foot" (1x12x12 inches). One board foot equals the surface area of one square foot, with a nominal thickness of one inch.

Wood is marketed by "grade." For most building projects No. 2 grade will satisfy your needs. This grade may have some blemishes, such as loose knots, but these don't reduce the strength of the wood.

If you're planning to build a unit that will be part of a room's decor, you should buy *select lumber*—a grade that's relatively free of blemishes.

Remember, too, that outdoor projects are a different subject.

Redwood or cedar is preferable, but if you use a soft wood such as fir, be sure to treat it for moisture resistance.

You can buy boards up to 16 feet in length and 12 inches in width, though occasionally a lumberyard may have somewhat wider or longer boards.

Wood is divided into two categories. Softwoods, used commonly for general construction, come from trees that don't shed their leaves in the winter: hemlock, fir, pine, spruce, and similar evergreen cone-bearing trees. Hardwoods come from trees that do shed their leaves: maple, oak, birch, mahogany, walnut, and other broad-leaved varieties.

All lumber is sold by a nominal size. A 2x4, for example, does not measure two by four inches. It's actually 1½x3½ inches (though the nominal *length* of a 2x4 is usually its true length). The drawing shows nominal sizes, as well as the actual sizes, of most pieces of common lumber.

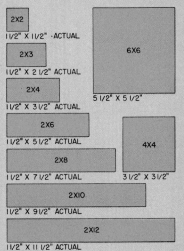

STANDARD LUMBER SIZES

1X2 — 3/4" X 1 1/2" ACTUAL
1X3 — 3/4" X 2 1/2" ACTUAL
1X4 — 3/4" X 3 1/2" ACTUAL
1X5 — 3/4" X 4 1/2" ACTUAL
1X6 — 3/4" X 5 1/2" ACTUAL
1X8 — 3/4" X 7 1/2" ACTUAL
1X10 — 3/4" X 9 1/2" ACTUAL
1X12 — 3/4" X 11 1/2" ACTUAL

4X6 — 3 1/2" X 5 1/2"
3X4 — 2 1/2" X 3 1/2"

2X2 — 1 1/2" X 1 1/2" ACTUAL
2X3 — 1 1/2" X 2 1/2" ACTUAL
2X4 — 1 1/2" X 3 1/2" ACTUAL
2X6 — 1 1/2" X 5 1/2" ACTUAL
2X8 — 1 1/2" X 7 1/2" ACTUAL
2X10 — 1 1/2" X 9 1/2" ACTUAL
2X12 — 1 1/2" X 11 1/2" ACTUAL

6X6 — 5 1/2" X 5 1/2"
4X4 — 3 1/2" X 3 1/2"

WOOD JOINERY TECHNIQUES

No matter what material you're planning to use, it will have to be cut to size—measure twice and cut once is a good rule—then put together using glue, nails or screws, and one of these joints.

Butt Joints

The simplest joint of all, the butt joint, consists of two pieces of wood meeting at a right angle and

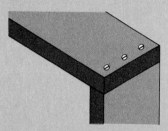

held together with nails, or preferably, screws (see sketch). A dab of glue before using the nails or screws will make the joint even more secure. But don't use glue if you're planning to take the work apart sometime later.

When reinforced by one of the six methods illustrated, the butt joint is effective for making corner

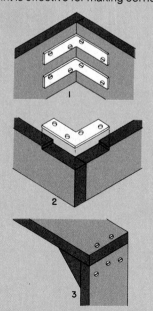

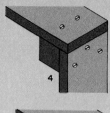

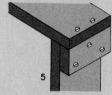

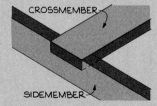

joints. Two common fasteners are angle irons (1), and flat corner plates (2). Using scrap wood, you can reinforce the joint with a triangular wedge (3), or with a square block (4). A variation of the square block places the block on the outside of the joint (5). Finally, a triangular gusset made from plywood or hardboard will also serve to reinforce a corner butt joint (6).

When a butt joint is in the form of a T—for example, in making a framework for light plywood or hardboard—you can reinforce it with an angle iron, T plate, or corrugated fasteners.

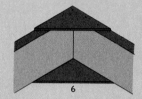

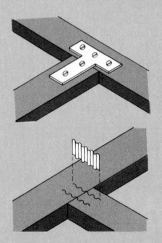

For really rough work, you can drive in a couple of nails at an

angle, or toenail (see sketch). A variation of this is to place a block of wood alongside the crosspiece

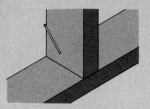

and secure it with a couple of nails.

A close cousin to the T joint and the butt joint is the plain overlap joint. It is held in place with at least two screws (see sketch). For extra reinforcement, apply glue between the pieces of wood.

Butt joints are an excellent means of securing backs to various units, especially when appearance is not a factor. Simply cut the back to the outside di-

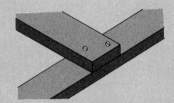

mensions of the work, then nail in place . . . it's called a flush back.

Lap Joints

On those projects where appearance is vital, consider full and half-lap joints. To make a full lap joint, cut a recess in one of the pieces of wood equal in depth to the thickness of the crossmember (see sketch).

The half-lap joint is similar to the full lap joint when finished, but the technique is different. First, cut a recess equal to half the

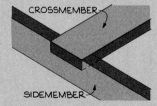

thickness of the crossmember halfway through the crossrail. Then, make a similar cut in the opposite half of the other piece (see sketch on the next page).

Butt joints and overlap joints do

not require any extra work besides cutting the pieces to size. However, full and half-lap joints

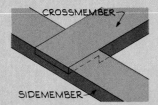

require the use of a backsaw and a chisel. For a full-lap joint, mark off the thickness and width of the crossmember on the work in which it is to fit.

Use the backsaw to make a cut at each end that's equal to the thickness of the crossmember, then use a chisel to remove the wood between the backsaw cuts. Check for sufficient depth and finish off with a fine rasp or sandpaper. Apply white glue to the mating surfaces and insert two screws to hold the joint securely.

Dado Joints

The dado joint is a simple way of suspending a shelf from its side supports. To make a dado joint, draw two parallel lines with a knife

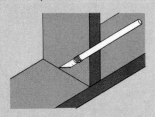

across the face of the work equal to the thickness of the wood it is to engage (see sketch). The depth should be about one-third of the thickness of the wood.

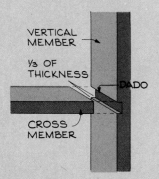

Next, make cuts on these lines and one or more between the lines

with a backsaw. Then, chisel out the wood to the correct depth.

You can speed the job immeasurably by using a router, a bench saw, or a radial arm saw. Any one of these power tools makes the cutting of dadoes an easy job — and provides much greater accuracy than can be achieved by hand.

If appearance is a factor, consider the stopped dado joint. In this type of joint, the dado (the cutaway part) extends only part way, and only a part of the shelf is cut away to match the non-cut part of the dado.

To make a stopped dado, first make your guide marks and chisel away a small area at the stopped end to allow for saw movement. Then make saw cuts

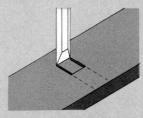

along your guide marks to the proper depth. Next chisel out the waste wood as shown in sketch.

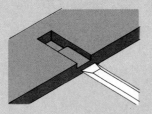

And finally, cut away a corner of the connecting board to accommodate the stopped dado.

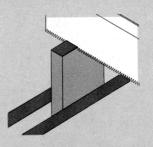

Rabbet Joints

The rabbet joint is really a partial dado. As you can see in the drawing at the top of the following column, only one of the meet-

ing members is cut away.

The rabbet joint is a simple one to construct, and it's quite strong, too. To ensure adequate strength, be sure to secure the meeting members with nails or screws and glue.

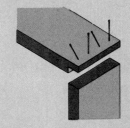

This joint is often used in the construction of inset backs for units such as cabinets and bookshelves (see the sketch below). To make this joint, rabbet each of the framing members, then care-

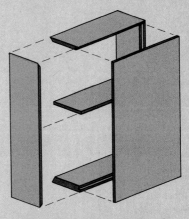

fully measure the distance between the rabbeted openings. Cut the back accordingly. Then use thin screws to secure the back to the unit.

Mortise and Tenon Joints

A particularly strong joint, the mortise and tenon joint is excellent when used for making T joints, right-angle joints, and for joints in the middle of rails. As its name indicates, this joint has two

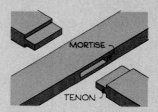

parts—the *mortise,* which is the open part of the joint, and the *tenon,* the part that fits into the mortise.

Make the mortise first, as it is much easier to fit the tenon to the mortise than the other way around. Divide the rail (the part to be mortised) into thirds and carefully mark off the depth and the width of the opening with a sharp pencil.

Next, use a chisel, equal to the width of the mortise, to remove the wood between the pencil marks. You can expedite this job by drilling a series of holes in the rail with an electric drill, a drill press, or even a hand drill. (If you have a drill press, you can purchase a special mortising bit that will drill square holes, believe it or not.) Mark the drill bit with a bit of tape to indicate the desired depth. Now use the chisel to remove the excess wood.

To make the tenon, divide the rail into thirds, mark the required depth, and use a backsaw to remove unwanted wood. If you have a bench or radial saw, the job of removing the wood will be much easier. Use a dado blade and set the blades high enough to remove the outer third of the wood. Reverse the work and remove the lower third, leaving the inner third intact.

To assemble, make a trial fit, and if all is well, apply some white glue to the tenon and insert it into the mortise. If by chance the tenon is too small for the mortise, simply insert hardwood wedges at top and bottom.

Use moderate clamping pressure on the joint until the glue dries overnight. Too much pressure will squeeze out the glue, actually weakening the joint.

Miter Joints

You can join two pieces of wood meeting at a right angle rather elegantly with a miter joint. And it's not a difficult joint to make. All you need is a miter box and a backsaw, or a power saw that you can adjust to cut at a 45 degree angle.

Since the simple miter joint is a surface joint with no shoulders for support, you must reinforce it. The easiest way to do this is with nails and glue (see sketch at the top of the following column). You'll notice that most picture

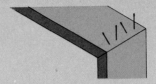

frames are made this way.

However, for cabinet and furniture work, you may use other means of reinforcement. One way is to use a hardwood spline as shown in the drawing. Apply glue to the spline and to the mitered

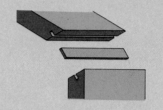

area and clamp as shown until the glue dries.

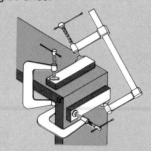

A variation of the long spline uses several short splines—at least three—inserted at opposing angles.

Dowels are a popular method of reinforcing a mitered joint, too. Careful drilling of the holes is necessary to make certain the dowel holes align. Use dowels that are slightly shorter than the holes they are to enter to allow for glue at the bottom. Score or roughen the

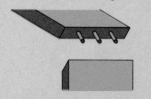

dowels to give the glue a better surface for a strong bond.

Dovetail Joints

The dovetail joint is a sign of good craftsmanship. It's a strong joint especially good for work subject

to heavy loads.

To make the joint, first draw the outline of the pin as shown and

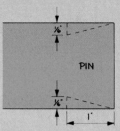

cut away the excess wood with a sharp backsaw. Place the pin over the second piece of wood and draw its outline with a sharp pencil. Make the two side cuts with the backsaw and an additional cut or two to facilitate the next step—chiseling away the excess wood. Then test for fit, apply glue and clamp the pieces until

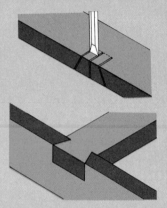

dry. This is the basic way to make most dovetail joints. However, it's much easier to make dovetail joints with a router and dovetail template, especially made for home craftsman use.

Corner Joints

These joints are used for attaching legs to corners for framing. A good technique for joining corners is the three-way joint involving a set of steel braces you can buy. First, insert the bolt into the inside corner of the leg. Then cut slots into the side members, and secure the brace with two screws at each end. Finally, tighten the wing nut.

A variation of the three-way joint uses dowels and a triangular ¾-inch-thick gusset plate for additional reinforcement. To make this joint, first glue the dowels in

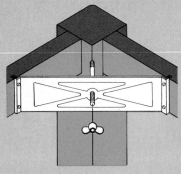

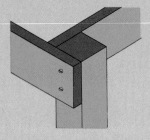

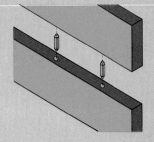

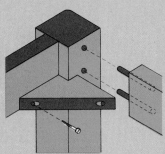

the vertical piece (see sketch). Let them dry completely, then finish the assembly.

A glued miter joint, reinforced with screws and glue, also makes a good corner joint. Make sure the screws do not penetrate the outside surface of the mitered joint.

Probably the strongest of the corner joints is the mortise and tenon (with mitered ends) reinforced with screws (see sketch). The miters on the ends of the tenons allow for a buildup of glue in the mortise, which in turn makes the joint stronger. Make sure that the holes you drill for the screws are not in line with each other.

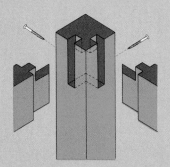

Otherwise, the wood may split. Use flathead screws and countersink the holes.

The simplest corner joint of all is a butt joint for the two horizontal members (see sketch). Instead

of being fastened to each other, the butted members are each

fastened to the corner post with screws.

Edge-to-Edge Joints

Whenever an extra-wide surface is required, such as a desk top, workbench, or a large storage cabinet, this joint fills the bill. To make it, glue together two or more boards, then hold securely with either bar or pipe clamps. If the boards have a pronounced grain, reverse them side-to-side

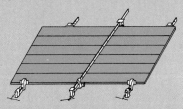

to minimize warping. For additional strength, screw cleats to the underside of the boards.

You also can use hardwood splines to join several boards. Cut a groove the exact width of the spline along the meeting sides of the two boards (see sketch). Cut the grooves slightly deeper than the spline width and in the exact center of the board thickness. The best way to cut such grooves is with a router or a bench saw.

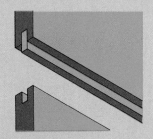

Then assemble with glue and clamps.

Another possibility for joining several boards involves the use of dowels. To make this joint, first

make holes in the boards. You can either use a doweling jig or a drill. If you use a drill, first drive

brads (small finishing nails) into one board and press them against the second board to leave marks for drilling. Make the dowel holes slightly deeper than the dowels. Score the dowels, apply glue, join the two boards together, and clamp with pipe or bar clamps until the glue sets (allow plenty of time).

If you'll be drilling many dowel holes, you may want to use a wood or metal template to ensure accurate spacing.

Box Joints

One joint is so common in the construction of boxes — and drawers — it's called a *box joint,* or a *finger joint because its parts* look like the outstretched fingers of a hand (see sketch). Note that one of the mating pieces must have two end fingers, or one more

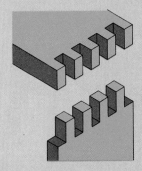

finger than the piece it is to engage. You can make this joint by hand with a backsaw and a small, sharp chisel. However, it is much easier, quicker, and more accurate to make it on a bench saw. Use a dado blade set to the desired width and proper depth of the fingers and mark off the waste area so there will be no mistake as to what you want to cut away.

SUPPORT SYSTEMS

Any item you construct, no matter how light, must be capable of supporting itself as well as its "payload". Even a simple box has a support system: its sides are self-supporting, each one serving to support and strengthen its neighbor.

How to Attach Things to Walls

Many items, such as shelves and wall-hung cabinets, depend on the wall as part of their support system. However, you can't always drive a nail or insert a screw just anywhere in a wall. For best stability, drive them into the studs of the wall.

Locating studs. One way of locating wall studs is to rap the wall with your knuckles. Listen for a "solid" sound. (Thumps between the studs will sound hollow.) This works fine if you have excellent hearing.

A far easier way is to buy an inexpensive stud finder. Its magnetic needle will respond to hidden nails, indicating the presence of a stud.

Locating one stud does not necessarily mean that the next stud is 16 inches away, though. It should be, but many times it isn't. For example, if the framework of a door or wall falls 20 inches away from the last stud, the builder may have left a 20-inch gap between them. Or, a stud may have been placed midway, leaving 10-inch spaces on either side.

Fastening to hollow-core walls. Quite often, because of physical requirements, you will need to make an installation between studs into a hollow plaster wall.

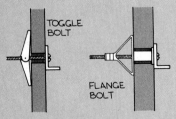
TOGGLE BOLT
FLANGE BOLT

What then? The answer is to use flange or toggle bolts. They distribute their load over a wide area,

and if used in sufficient number and with discretion, they'll hold a fairly heavy load.

Fastening to masonry. Attaching items to a masonry wall is not difficult. if you're working with a brick, concrete, or cinder block wall, use a carbide-tipped drill to make a hole *in the mortar*. Make the hole deep and wide enough to accept a wall plug. Then insert the screw or bolt to fasten the item in place (see sketch).

Another method of fastening to

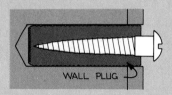
WALL PLUG

masonry walls is to drill a ½-inch hole in the *mortar* and pound a hardwood dowel into the hole. Bevel the end of the dowel and lightly coat it with grease before driving it in place. Then drill a pilot hole in the middle of the dowel and continue with the fastening.

If by chance you must drill into the brick part of a wall rather than the mortar, don't despair. Again use a carbide-tipped drill, but this time start with a ¼-inch bit, and finish with the larger size desired.

How to Mount Units On a Base

If your project is any type of cabinet, a base is a good idea. A base should provide toe space of at least 3½ inches in height and 2¾ inches in depth. If you plan to mount the unit on casters, you'll automatically get toe space that makes the project convenient.

Box base. This easy-to-build recessed base consists of a four-sided open box installed at the

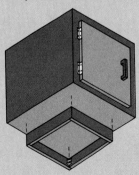

bottom of the cabinet or storage unit. Since appearance is not a factor, you can construct the box with simple butt joints and secure it to the cabinet with steel angle brackets installed along the inside of the base (see sketch).

Leg base. Four short, stubby legs also make a good base. Commercial legs come with their own mounting plate, which is screwed to the bottom of the cabinet before the leg is screwed into place (see sketch). You can also install home-built legs with hanger bolts.

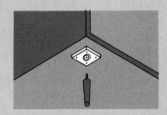

These bolts have a "wood" thread on one end and a coarse "machine" thread on the other end. Drill an undersize hole in the cabinet for the machine end, insert the hanger bolt using pliers and screw the leg into place.

A good source for low-priced legs is a lumberyard that does millwork. Quite often, they'll have a bin full of legs of all sizes that may have slight imperfections or chips which won't affect their serviceability.

How to Mount Shelves

Shelves are a quick and easy way of getting additional storage space in your home, shop, or garage. The best material for shelving is ¾-inch plywood or pine boards—8, 10, 12 inches wide, depending on the items to be stored. To prevent sagging, install a shelf support every 30 inches. And don't use hardboard or chip board, as they tend to bow under heavy loads.

STEEL SHELF BRACKET

Shelf brackets. The easiest way to mount a shelf is by means of steel shelf brackets sold in hardware stores (see sketch). Ask for brackets whose short leg is nearly equal to the *width* of the shelf you plan to install. And always mount the brackets with the *long* leg against the wall. Screw the brackets into the wall and space them about 30 inches apart. For heavy loads, shop around for brackets that have gussets connecting the two legs. Brackets without gussets tend to sway under heavy loads.

Cleats and angle brackets. The narrow space between two walls is an ideal location for shelving. Simply install a pair of cleats at the heights where you want shelves (see sketch). Use cleats that are at least ¾ inch thick and as long as the shelf is wide.

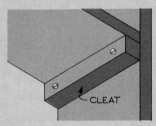

If the walls are of masonry, secure the cleats with so-called steel cut nails (wear goggles when driving these, as they may break off if not struck head-on). Secure the cleats with screws if the walls are of wood, or use flange bolts if they're hollow.

You can also use small steel angle brackets. Mount two under each side of the shelf as shown.

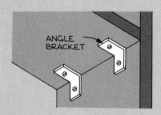

Dowels. Another method of supporting shelves is with dowels. Drill holes equal to the diameter of the dowels, and bore them deep enough to accept at least ½-inch of dowel length. (Make sure both left and right holes are the same height; you might use a level on the shelves to ensure exact mounting.)

Use ¼-inch dowels for light-duty shelves and ⅜-inch dowels for shelves supporting heavy loads. Beveling the dowel ends

will make them easier to insert into the holes. To change shelf spacing, simply drill additional holes.

Dado cuts. This method of supporting shelves has long been a favorite with master cabinetmakers. First, determine the height of the shelf, mark the uprights, and make your cuts. Then cut the shelf to fit.

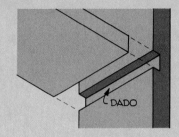

Metal tracks and brackets. You can recess or surface-mount these handy shelf supports. Shelf brackets, specially designed to fit into the track slots, are made to accept 8-, 10-, and 12-inch-wide shelves. Special brackets which adjust to hold shelves at a downward slope also are available and are used to hold dictionaries and reference books.

These tracks and brackets are available in finishes to match the decor of practically any room.

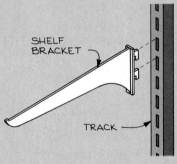

When installing shelves in a cabinet, mount two tracks on each side of the cabinet and use small clips to hold the shelves in place. To change the spacing between shelves, just remove the clips and reposition.

Furring strips. These are especially useful for supporting and erecting shelves in the garage or workshop. Use 2x4s bolted or screwed to the wall and short lengths of 1x4s for shelf supports, as indicated in the drawing. Note that one end is dadoed into the 2x4 (½-inch depth is enough). The

front end of the shelf support bracket is supported by a 1x2 cut at a 45 degree angle at the bottom and engages a cutout called a *bird's mouth* at the top. Toenail

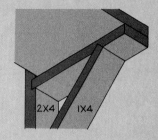

the lower end of the 1x2 into the 2x4. There's no need to nail the upper end, as the weight of the shelf will keep it in place.

Support from above. While most shelves are supported from the bottom, you can also support them from the top. This top support method is especially applicable in basement areas where the joists are exposed. You can nail 2x4s to the joists and fit any type of

project—open shelves, a cabinet, even a work surface between them. If the project to be suspended will run perpendicular to the joists, be careful to plan the length so that it will match the spacing of the joists.

Another way to support shelving from the top is use threaded rods (see sketch above). Choose rods from ¼- to ¾-inch diameter according to the load you'll support. Drill holes in the shelves slightly oversize. To attach the upper end of the rod, drill holes in 2x2 scraps and screw to the joists. Insert the rod and add a nut and washer to the top.

Then install the shelves with a nut and washer on both top and bottom. Tighten the nuts securely to give the shelves as much stability as possible.

HOW TO MAKE DRAWERS

Next to shelves, drawers are the most convenient place for storage. And a drawer is comparatively easy to build. It's just a five-sided box, connected at its corners with the joints previously described.

Types of Drawers

Drawers, no matter how they're made, fall into two general classifications—the flush or recessed type, and the lip type.

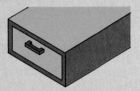

Flush drawers. You must fit this type of drawer carefully to the cabinet opening, with only enough clearance at top and sides to facilitate sliding in and out. In fact, some custom cabinetmakers often will make flush-type drawers with a taper of 1/16 inch from front to back to ensure a good appearance and an easy-sliding fit.

Lipped drawers. These drawers have an oversize front panel that completely covers the drawer opening and so offers much greater leeway in fitting the drawer into its recess.

One way to make a lipped drawer is to rabbet the front panel to the sides and bottom of the drawer, leaving an overlap of ½ inch or so. A simpler way is to screw a false front to the finished drawer front. With this method, if there is any error in construction, the false front will hide it. Attach the drawer front with countersunk flathead screws from the *inside* of the drawer. In addition to the screws, apply white glue between the two pieces.

Construction Details

When making drawers, remember to make the cabinet first, then fit the drawers to the cabinet openings. To make a drawer, first determine its length and cut two pieces of wood to this size and the required width. (The width, of course, will be the height of the finished drawer.)

Draw two parallel lines, equal to the thickness of the drawer back, about ½ inch from the ends

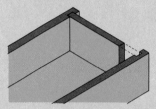

of the two pieces. Cut a dado between these lines to a depth of ¼ inch.

Next, measure the inside distance between the two sides of the drawer opening and cut the drawer back to this measurement. (Allow for clearance and the depth of the dado cuts in the drawer sides.)

For the front of the drawer, plan simple butt joints and cut it to allow a ¼-inch overhang on all sides, if you plan a lip.

You are now ready to partially assemble the drawer. Brush some white glue into the two dado cuts and install the back panel. Use three or four brads at each joint to secure the sides. Next attach the drawer front using glue and brads or screws to secure it to the sides.

A false front nailed or screwed to the existing front from the inside of the drawer will conceal the original brads or screws. If you use brads, countersink them with a nail set.

The bottom of the drawer consists of ¼-inch or thicker plywood, and is nailed to the sides and back of the drawer. For stronger, more elaborate construction, you can use any one of the woodworking joints described earlier in this section.

Drawer Runners and Guides

To ensure that the drawers you build will move in and out without wobbling, you can use any one of three methods: guides located at each side of the drawer; a central guide placed at the bottom of the drawer; or commercial metal tracks mounted on the sides of the cabinet with nylon wheels on the drawer sides. These come in lengths to fit most drawers and are especially good for heavy loads. Select them before you build the drawer in order to plan the clearance space.

The simplest guide consists of two narrow lengths of wood secured to each side of the drawer, spaced an inch apart (see sketch). Another strip of wood, mounted on each side of the

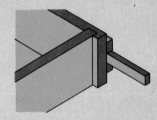

drawer opening, fits the "track" mounted on the drawer sides. To ease operation, apply paste wax to all touching surfaces.

For guides at the bottom of the drawer, mount lengths of wood on the cabinet and engage the two strips of wood on the bottom of the drawer.

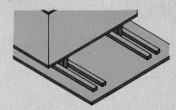

If you're planning to incorporate runners and guides in the drawers, make allowances before starting work. A clearance of ½-inch is required for guides mounted at the sides of the drawers, and 1 inch for center-mounted guides. Regardless of what type of drawer guides you use, make sure you install them accurately.

You can even make easy-sliding drawers without guides or runners by installing plastic glides in the drawer openings so the bottom of the drawer will bear against plastic instead of wood. Steel thumbtacks also ease drawer movement. But don't forget to apply wax to the bottom bearing surfaces of the drawer.

HOW TO INSTALL CABINET DOORS

Except for shelves, tables, and chairs, nearly every piece of furniture you build will have some sort of door. All doors require hinges or tracks, and handles for opening and closing. Here are the basics.

Construction Pointers

To prevent warping, cabinet doors should be at least ½ inch thick. However, you can use a ¼-inch panel, providing you frame it with ½-inch wood, somewhat like a picture frame.

If you plan to laminate a door panel with plastic, use the thin grade laminate especially made for vertical surfaces. The heavy grade, made for countertops, may cause the cabinet to warp.

Sliding Doors

Sliding doors are easier to fit and install than swinging doors, and, as a rule, are of much lighter stock than conventional doors. Track for sliding doors can be aluminum or plastic (left sketch), or it can consist of grooves cut into the top and bottom of the framework (right sketch).

Of course, you must cut these grooves before assembly. Make the upper grooves about twice as deep as the bottom ones so you can lift up, then lower the door into place. The doors should be flush with the bottom shelf surface when it's touching the top of the upper groove.

To ease sliding, apply wax or a silicone spray to the grooves. If you're planning to use handles, recess them into the door so there will be no interference when the doors bypass each other.

Hinged Doors

Flush-type hinged doors that recess within the framing require clearance all around to prevent binding. To install a flush-type door, make a dry fit, and if the door fits, insert small wedges at all sides to hold it in place and ensure clearance until the hinges have been completely installed.

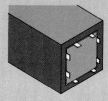

Then place the hinge against the door—if it's an exterior mounting—and mark the hinge holes with an awl. Drill pilot holes and install the hinges. Use this same procedure if you have an interior mounting job.

With hinges that are partly concealed—half on the inside of the door and half on the frame—mount the hinges on the door first, set the door in place, and mark the location of the hinge on the frame or door jamb. This method is much easier than trying to fit an already-mounted hinge to the blind or interior part of the door.

Types of hinges. There are literally dozens of types of hinges to choose from. Following are a few of the more common varieties.

As a general rule, you should mortise hinges into cabinets so they are flush with the work. However, always surface mount decorative hinges, such as colonial, rustic, and ornamental hinges.

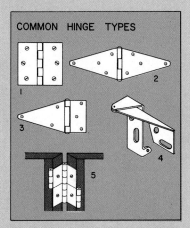

COMMON HINGE TYPES

(1) *Butt hinges* are the type you're probably most familiar with. Use them for either right- or left-hand doors. The larger sizes have re-movable pins to facilitate taking off the door; the smaller sizes don't. For long cabinet doors or lids. use a piano hinge (a long butt hinge) rather than several smaller ones. (2, 3) The *strap hinge* and the *T hinge* are used for extra-heavy doors. There's no need to mortise these hinges, as they are strictly functional.

(4) *Pivot hinges,* also called knife hinges, are available in different shapes and are especially good for use on ¾-inch plywood doors. All shapes present a very unobtrusive appearance.

(5) *Double-acting hinges* allow a door to be swung from either direction.

Self-closing hinges operate by means of a spring concealed within the barrel of the hinge. Another type, used on kitchen cabinets, has no spring, yet closes the door with a positive snapping action. Its secret is a square shoulder next to the pin.

Special-purpose hinges are available with offset leaves (so the door will overlap the framing); hinges with knuckles (for quick door removal); ball-bearing hinges lubricated for life (for extra-heavy doors); hinges that will automatically raise a door when it is opened (so that it will clear a carpet on the far side of the door); burglar-resistant hinges (with pins that can't be removed when they're on the outside); and hinges that allow a door to be swung back far enough so that the full width of the doorway can be utilized.

Door catches and handles. In addition to hinges, you will need hardware to keep the doors closed and to lock them. For cabinet work, your best hardware bets are spring-loaded or magnetic catches.

Spring-loaded catches come with single and double rollers and are ideal for lipped doors, flush doors, double doors, and shelves. These catches are adjustable.

Install magnetic catches so there is physical contact between the magnet in the frame and the "keeper" on the door.

A handle of some type is required for all drawers and doors. Handles can be surface-mounted or recessed flush with the drawer or door. Sliding doors always use recessed handles so the doors can bypass each other.

THE HARDWARE YOU'LL NEED

For any sort of fastening work, you will need nails, screws, and bolts, as well as glues and cements.

Nails, Screws, and Bolts

These most common of all fastening materials are available in diverse widths and lengths, and in steel, brass, aluminum, copper, and even stainless steel.

Nails. Nails are sold by the penny—which has nothing to do with their cost. The "penny," (abbreviated *d*) refers to the size. The chart shows a box nail marked in the penny size designations as well as actual lengths in inches.

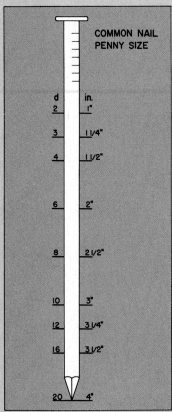

d	in.
2	1"
3	1 1/4"
4	1 1/2"
6	2"
8	2 1/2"
10	3"
12	3 1/4"
16	3 1/2"
20	4"

COMMON NAIL PENNY SIZE

Use common nails for general-purpose work; finish and casing nails for trim or cabinetwork; and brads for attaching molding to walls and furniture.

COMMON SCREWS

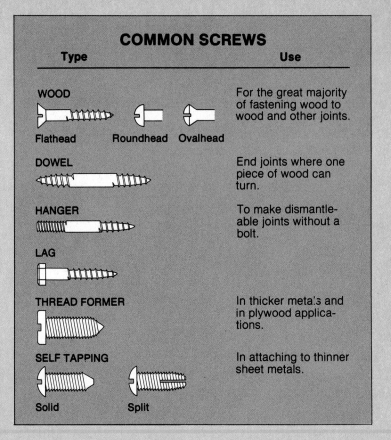

Type	Use
WOOD Flathead Roundhead Ovalhead	For the great majority of fastening wood to wood and other joints.
DOWEL	End joints where one piece of wood can turn.
HANGER	To make dismantle-able joints without a bolt.
LAG	
THREAD FORMER	In thicker metals and in plywood applications.
SELF TAPPING Solid Split	In attaching to thinner sheet metals.

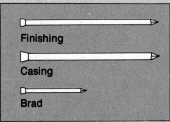

Finishing

Casing

Brad

Screws. Screws are sold by length and diameter. The diameter is indicated by a number, from 1 to 16. The thicker the screw shank, the larger the number. The drawing shows some of the most popular types of screws.

Always drill a pilot hole when inserting a screw into hardwood. And always drill a clearance hole in the leading piece of wood when screwing two pieces of wood together. Without a clearance hole, the leading piece tends to "hang up," preventing a tight fit between the two.

Bolts. You can also fasten wood together with bolts, but only if there is access to the back for the required washer and nut. A bolted joint is stronger than a screwed joint, as the bolt diameter is generally thicker than the comparable screw, and also because the wrench used to tighten the nut can apply much more force than a screwdriver in a screw slot.

Glues and Cements

While not "hardware" as such, glue is an important adjunct to any fastening job. The so-called white glue is excellent for use with wood, and only moderate clamping pressure is required. When dry, it is crystal clear. However, it's not waterproof so don't use it for work subject to excessive dampness—and of course, never for outdoor use. Use the two-tube epoxy "glue" for joints that must be waterproof.

Plastic resin glue, a powder that you mix with water to a creamy consistency, is highly water resistant.

Contact cement provides an excellent bond between wood and wood, and wood and plastic. When working with contact cement, remember that it dries instantly and position your surfaces

COMMON BOLTS

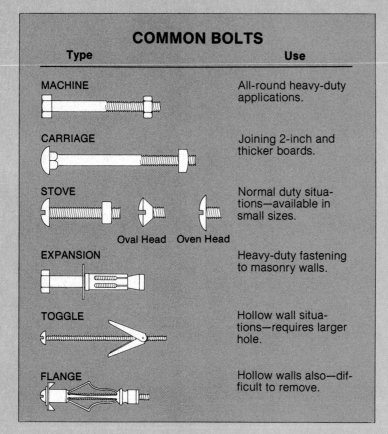

Type	Use
MACHINE	All-round heavy-duty applications.
CARRIAGE	Joining 2-inch and thicker boards.
STOVE (Oval Head, Oven Head)	Normal duty situations—available in small sizes.
EXPANSION	Heavy-duty fastening to masonry walls.
TOGGLE	Hollow wall situations—requires larger hole.
FLANGE	Hollow walls also—difficult to remove.

The plate type caster is merely screwed to the bottom by four screws that pass through holes in the plate. They are not height adjustable unless, of course, you use shims.

All casters use ball bearings as part of the plate assembly to facilitate swiveling. For extra-heavy usages, purchase casters with ball-bearing wheels as well.

The wheels on casters are of two types—plastic or rubber. Use casters with plastic wheels if the project is to be rolled on a soft surface such as a rug; rubber wheeled casters are best on hard concrete, vinyl, or hardwood. It's a good idea to use graphite to lubricate the wheels and their bearings, as oil tends to pick up dust and dirt.

To prevent a caster-equipped unit from rolling, get locking casters. A small lever on the outside of the wheel locks a "brake." Brakes on only two of the four casters on a unit are sufficient.

When to Use What Glue

Type	Use
White glue (No mixing)	Paper, cloth, wood
Epoxy (requires mixing)	Wood, metal, stone (waterproof)
Plastic resin (requires mixing)	Wood to wood (water resistant)
Contact cement (no mixing)	Wood to wood or plastic (waterproof)
Waterproof glue (requires mixing)	Wood to wood (waterproof)

together exactly as you want them. You won't get a second chance.

True waterproof glue comes in two containers; one holds a liquid resin, the other a powder catalyst. When dry, this glue is absolutely waterproof and can be safely used for garden equipment and all outdoor projects and furniture.

Glides and Casters

The intended use determines whether a piece of furniture needs a caster or a glide. If you don't plan to move it frequently, use a glide; otherwise, a caster is the best choice.

Glides come in many sizes, determined by the glide area touching the floor, and with steel or plastic bottoms. The simple nail-on glides aren't height adjustable but you can adjust screw glides by screwing the glide in or out to prevent wobbling if the floor is uneven, or if by some chance, the project does not have an even base.

Casters are made in two styles—stem type (only the stem type is adjustable) and plate type (at left in sketch). The stem type requires a hole to be drilled into the leg or base of the cabinet or furniture. This hole accepts a sleeve that in turn accepts the stem of the caster.

Miscellaneous Hardware

There are many types of hardware that can come in handy when you're constructing storage bins, cabinets, chests, shelves, and other projects.

Following are some you may need from time to time: corrugated fasteners connect two boards or mend splits in wood; angle irons reinforce corners; flat and T plates also reinforce work; masonry nails secure work to concrete or brick walls; steel plates with a threaded center are used for attaching legs to cabinets; screw eyes and cup hooks allow for hanging items inside storage units; and lag screw plugs made of lead or plastic secure furring strips or shelf brackets to masonry walls.

You'll be wise to stock your workshop with most of these items in a couple of sizes. That way, you won't have to make a special trip when they're needed.

FINISHING TECHNIQUES

Finishing is your final job before you can step back and admire your work. Before starting, make sure that all nails are flush or countersunk and filled, all flathead screws are flush with the surface, all cracks are filled, and all surfaces are sanded and cleaned.

Hardboard and Chip Board

If the unit you have built is made of hardboard, about the only finish you can apply to it is paint. No preparation is needed except to remove any oil or dirt. Inasmuch as hardboard is brown—the tempered type is a darker brown—you'll need to apply at least two coats of paint if you want the final finish to be a light color.

Hardboard will accept latex or alkyd paints equally well. Between coats, let dry overnight and then sand lightly.

You also can paint chip board, flake board, and particle board, but because of their slightly rougher texture you should apply a "filler" coat of shellac first, then proceed with painting.

Plywood

Because of its comparatively low cost, fir plywood is used extensively for building projects. However, the hard and soft growth patterns in the wood will show through unless a sealer is used before painting or finishing with varnish or lacquer.

After sealing, sand lightly and finish with at least two coats of paint, varnish, or lacquer. The final step for varnish or lacquer work consists of an application of paste wax applied with fine steel wool and polishing with terry cloth or any other coarse-textured cloth.

Plywood has a pronounced end grain due to its layered construction. If your project will be on display, it's best to hide the end grain, and there are several ways to do this.

A mitered joint is the obvious solution, as then the end grain is hidden within the joint. Another

solution is wood veneer tape (see sketch). This tape comes in rolls and is really walnut, oak, mahogany, or a similar wood in a very thin strip about ¾ inch wide. Either glue it or use contact cement, applying the cement to the tape and to the plywood edges. When the cement has lost its gloss, carefully align the tape and press over the plywood edge.

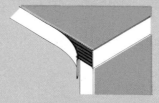

You also can use molding to cover the edges. It has the additional advantage of making a decorative edge requiring no further treatment.

Metal molding is another option, especially useful for edges which are subject to wear and abuse.

A rabbet joint will also hide end grain. Make the rabbet deep enough so that only the last ply is uncut.

Other Woods

If your project is constructed of a fine wood, a more elaborate finishing technique is needed.

Sanding. You can do this by hand or with a power sander. A power belt sander is fine for initial sanding, but always do the final sanding with an orbital or straight line finishing sander—or with fine sandpaper.

Filling and staining. Open grain woods such as oak, chestnut, walnut, ash, and mahogany require a filler to close their pores. Apply the filler with a brush or rag, wiping across the grain. After 10 or 15 minutes, remove the excess filler with a coarse cloth.

If a stain is called for, let the wood dry for 24 hours before application. A stain applied over a filler that has not dried will show up as a "hot" spot.

Sealing. A sealer, as its name implies, is used to seal the stains and filler from the subsequent finishing coats.

One of the best sealers is shellac. One advantage of using shellac is that it prevents the stain from bleeding. Thin the shellac with alcohol to the consistency of

light cream; as it comes in the can, it's much too thick for use as a sealer. You can also use ready-mixed stains combined with a sealer.

Finishes. *Varnish,* the traditional finish for wood, is available in many types and colors.

To prepare a piece for varnish, sand it lightly, wipe off the dust with a turpentine-dampened rag, and apply the varnish with long, flowing strokes. Do not brush out the varnish as you would paint. And don't use varnish during humid weather. To make sure the varnish will flow evenly, place the can in warm water.

Varnish requires at least two coats, with a minimum of 24 hours drying time. Sand lightly between coats. After the second or third coat has dried for at least a week, rub down with steel wool and paste wax. Polish with a rough cloth.

Shellac, too, will yield super results. It's fairly easy to work with and it dries dust free in a half-hour. You can apply the second coat within two hours. Sanding is not required between coats, as the second coat tends to partially dissolve and melt into the first one.

One disadvantage of shellac is that it shows a ring if a liquor-stained glass is placed on a shellac-finished surface. Also, shellac sometimes tends to crack if exposed to dampness.

Polyurethane is a tough synthetic varnish that resists abrasion, alcohol, and fruit stains. It's great for floors, furniture, walls, and woodwork. To apply polyurethane the surface must be clean, dry, and free of grease, oil, and wax. Don't apply a polyurethane finish over previously shellacked or lacquered surfaces. Allow at least 12 hours drying time for each coat, and clean your brushes with mineral spirits or turpentine.

Lacquer is a fast-drying finish you can apply by spray or brush. For spraying, thin lacquer only with lacquer thinner. *Never use turpentine or mineral spirits.*

To brush lacquer, always use a brush that has *never* been used to apply paint.

And never apply lacquer over a painted surface, as the lacquer will lift the paint. As with shellac, sanding between coats is not necessary.